The Works of Edmond Rostand

Also by Kay Nolte Smith

CHANTECLER

CHANTECLER

by EDMOND ROSTAND

A Play In Four Acts

Translated By

KAY NOLTE SMITH

Drawings for the cover, the frontispiece, and the Act pages
adapted by Joan Mitchell Blumenthal
from those in the original French edition.
End-of-act drawings reproduced from that edition.

Chantecler was dedicated by Rostand to his son Jean.
The play was first produced at the Théâtre de la Porte-Saint-Martin, Paris
on February 7, 1910

UNIVERSITY
PRESS OF
AMERICA

LANHAM • NEW YORK • LONDON

Copyright © 1987 by

University Press of America,® Inc.

4720 Boston Way
Lanham, MD 20706

3 Henrietta Street
London WC2E 8LU England

Printed in the United States of America

British Cataloging in Publication Information Available

Library of Congress Cataloging in Puublication Data

Rostand, Edmond, 1868-1918.
  Chantecler : a play in four acts.

  "Drawings . . . adapted by Joan Mitchell Blumenthal
from those in the original French edition."
  1. Roosters—Drama.   2. Birds—drama.   I. Title.
PQ2635.07C42   1987   842'.8   86-26799
ISBN 0-8191-5765-1 (alk. paper)
ISBN 0-8191-5766-X (pbk. : alk. paper)

All University Press of America books are produced on acid-free
paper which exceeds the minimum standards set by the National
Historical Publication and Records Commission.

To my mother, Sigrid Johnson Nolte, who taught me to love books, and my father, Cliff Nolte, who taught me how to read them.

PREFACE

Chantecler fits into no category. It is an animal fantasy, yes, but one whose purpose is to exalt mankind. It is a Romantic drama, yes, but one whose characters are busy with such things as pecking grain. Unique and audaciously imaginative, *Chantecler* portrays idealism in a barnyard, turns a rooster into a bravura Romantic hero, and puts lyric poetry into the mouths—rather, the beaks—of poultry.

There are no humans in *Chantecler*, but there are human values. The hero is a cock who believes his crowing makes the sun rise—who experiences not only the exaltation of the artist but also his struggle with mockery, self-doubt, and envy. The heroine is an "emancipated" pheasant—who offers love and then reveals its tyranny. Chantecler's enemies are Owls and other Nightbirds who plot to have him killed in an exotic cockfight—who envy his talent and hate him for his dedication to his ideal, the Light. Other writers have used the animal kingdom, as in *The Birds* and *Animal Farm*, but their goal has been to satirize human beings. Although *Chantecler* too has its satire—a literary cocktail party in Act Three is a biting attack on artistic trends—it is always secondary to the deeper purpose: to inspire. As Rostand said in his acceptance speech when he was elected to the French Academy (the youngest writer ever admitted):

> We want a theater where the auditors may be exalted by
> lyricism, morally influenced by beauty, consoled by grace,
> and where poets will give lessons of the soul.

Those were sentiments at odds with the literary times. Rostand was writing Romantic drama after the theater had turned against it, creating larger-than-life heroes as the theater was cutting life down to "slices." In fact, before *Cyrano de Bergerac* opened, all involved were so sure of a disastrous reception for an heroic play in verse that Rostand had to pay for the costumes himself. Fifteen minutes before the curtain went up on December 28, 1897, he was clinging to his friend Constant Coquelin, who played the title role, and begging pardon for having dragged him into such a scrape. The play was, of course, a stunning success. Rostand was hailed as the successor to Hugo, and the theater, otherwise committed to "thesis plays" and "naturalism" and every other form of rebellion it could devise against romanticism, lyricism, and melodrama, found one of its finest writers using a voice it had declared to be dead.

The success of *Cyrano*, followed by that of *L'Aiglon* in 1900, with Sarah Bernhardt in the title role, made the theater public of Paris, indeed of the world, avid for Rostand's next drama. They had to wait ten years for *Chantecler*.

The genesis of the play, Rostand explained, was nature herself. Out walking in the Basque country where he lived, he saw a blackbird hopping in a cage in a farmyard and seeming to gibe at a cock who entered the scene. Did the cock see the mockery? Rostand wondered. If so, what did he make of it? From that germ of comedy among animals Rostand created what he later described as "a drama of human effort grappling with life. Chantecler is man, confident in his work and refusing to let anything prevent him from accomplishing it." The play became his favorite among his works. The Cock "is the person I have used to express my own dreams," he wrote. "Chantecler is my God."

Chantecler opened in 1910, after a six-year delay during which it became the most eagerly anticipated theatrical event in the world. There were Chantecler fashions, toys, floats—even an "Eau de Coq" from Guerlain. The advance sale was an extraordinary (for the time) $200,000; people traveled from as far as America to attend; diplomats prolonged their stay to see it, making the French foreign minister complain that "diplomatic relations between France and many a foreign power are being interrupted all because of a cock and a hen pheasant."

The many postponements had various causes: Rostand's ill health, the difficulty of preparing the scenery and costumes (the former required props five times larger than lifesize, the latter a ton of feathers; thirty workers were kept busy on it all for nearly three years), and, heartbreakingly, the death of Coquelin, who was to have played Chantecler. Coquelin, whom Rostand called "the very incarnation of my superb, joyous, heroic, aggressive, noisy principal character as I had conceived him, carrying his crest high like the plume of Cyrano"; Coquelin, who so loved the play that he recited its key passages everywhere, making Rostand constantly reproach him for giving everything away (a South American journalist was caught at Rostand's estate attempting to steal a passage in manuscript; when Rostand asked, "Why? You don't even know what it's like," the man replied, "Oh, yes. M. Coquelin recited it to us in Argentina"); Coquelin, who died with *Chantecler* clutched in his hand— "the Coq" was irreplaceable yet had to be replaced. Lucien Guitry was the choice. Then, when the premiere was definitely scheduled at last, a huge flood turned parts of Paris into lakes and made people talk of going to *Chantecler* in gondolas. One can imagine the effect on the audience of the play's first words, uttered by the Manager of the Theater as he leaps to the stage to stop the curtain from rising: "Not yet!"

The reception did not equal the anticipation (as perhaps nothing could have). Although many praised the play's concept and beauty of language and it was eagerly exploited (in America, Maude Adams not only played it on Broadway but toured with it), there was not the ecstasy that had greeted *Cyrano*. Why? since Chantecler is, in many respects, a feathered Cyrano. Perhaps because animal characters are less accessible to audience. And almost certainly because the production was too realistic; rather than using stylized costumes and decor, it buried the actors in feathers and dwarfed them with scenery that, designed to give the birds' perspective, had to be huge.

In English, *Chantecler* has labored under an additional disadvantage. The lyricism and idealism that give the play its special character cannot be divorced from each other, yet one of the two previous English translations (1910) was in prose, and the other (1921) in verse that, despite some good passages, more often gave feet of lead to Rostand's muse. Having fallen in love with the French—with the splendor of Rostand's poetry, the wit of his word plays, and the exuberance of his imagination—I decided to attempt an English *Chantecler* that would recreate at least some measure of the wit and beauty of his language.

I also hoped to do some service, however small, to his reputation. Even though *Cyrano de Bergerac* has been on the boards somewhere in the world virtually since it opened—no character is more loved than the Gascon with the long nose and the great heart—even though the longest-running play in the American theater is based on one of Rostand's works (*The Fantasticks* is a musical version of his *Les Romanesques*), Rostand is persistently undervalued, often condescended to. Perhaps his spirit is too antithetical to the times. But perhaps, also, we simply need to know more of his work. And *Chantecler* is one of his masterpieces.

The original is written in Alexandrine rhymed couplets, with these passages in specific verse forms: the Prologue; the Ode to the Sun, Act One; the Nightbirds Chorus and the famous Hymn to the Sun, Act Two; the Prayer of the Birds and the Villanelle of the Toads and the Nightingale, Act Four. I translated those passages in rhyme, and throughout there are occasional rhymed couplets for emphasis. However, most of the translation is in blank verse (and is printed accordingly) because I believe that English rhymed couplets can grow deadly to read. My goal was to provide lyrical, rhythmic prose with highlights in rhyme—to create a text that could be read with pleasure. (And performed, if one of my greatest wishes is ever granted. May some American or English theater people who now discover the play find a way to bring it to life on the stage—perhaps in the form of a musical, to which it seems so well suited.)

To a degree, this translation is an adaptation. Because I wanted to preserve

Rostand's stated intention of creating a modern play, in which a barnyard would provide a meeting-ground for two usually incompatible elements—the contemporary and the lyrical—I updated references that now would make the play sound old-fashioned; wagons have become trucks, etc. In addition, I found English equivalents for uniquely French allusions, in order to make the play seem, not American, but also not specifically French (*pace* Rostand). For instance, although the cock is the national symbol of France, I have neither preserved that fact nor converted him into a "Yankee rooster." It may seem audacious to have stripped the national character from a play that is in many ways so specifically French, but I was supported in this approach by Rostand's son Jean, the distinguished biologist to whom the play was dedicated when he was a boy. M. Rostand wrote me that "to remain faithful to the spirit of the play. . . it would be better to remove it deliberately from its historical context without substituting another and to find again the fundamental inspiration; that is, the magic of the Word. For Chantecler is not only the Gallic Cock; even more, he is the one whose voice—I was going to say whose word—brings the light, all allowance being made, a little as in Genesis." (I am pleased that before his death M. Rostand read a third of this translation and was satisfied as to its quality.)

A word of caution to those not used to reading plays: It takes an effort of the imagination to plunge into the world of any dramatist, and perhaps even more so here. The best way to go is slowly, taking time to visualize what the stage directions suggest and to grow accustomed to dialogue in which lyric richness blends with the mundanities of barnyard life.

Whatever effort of imagination is required will, I think, be well repaid. For *Chantecler* not only provides wonderfully accurate observations of animal behavior—and of the human spirit—but offers qualities in short supply in modern drama: idealism, heroism, and lyricism. Those are hardly the "isms" of our theater, or of our times. Perhaps the theater, and the times, would be better if they were.

Personally, I shall always be grateful to *Chantecler*, for though the task of translation was long, demanding, and often maddeningly difficult, it was also exhilarating. One cannot spend time in Rostand's sun-drenched world without being warmed and lifted by his spirit.

Kay Nolte Smith
Tinton Falls, NJ
August 5, 1986

THE CHARACTERS

CHANTECLER
PATOU
THE BLACKBIRD
THE PEACOCK
THE GRAND DUKE
THE SCREECH OWL
SCOPS
THE FIGHTING COCK
THE HUNTING DOG
THE TURKEY
THE DUCK
THE GUINEA COCK
THE GANDER
A CAPON
THREE PULLETS
A YOUNG COCK
TWO PIGEON ACROBATS
THREE HOPPING CHICKENS
THE SWAN
THE MAGPIE USHER
THE CUCKOO
FIRST RABBIT
SECOND RABBIT
TWO CHICKS

THE NIGHTBIRDS

THE EXOTIC COCKS

THE TOADS

THE PHEASANT
THE GUINEA HEN
THE OLD HEN
THE WHITE HEN
THE GRAY HEN
THE BLACK HEN
THE SPECKLED HEN
THE MOLE
THE NIGHTINGALE
A SPIDER

The Barnyard Animals, the Beasts of the Forest, the Rabbits, the Birds, the Bees, the Wasps, the Cicadas, Voices.

PROLOGUE

The houselights dim. The curtain trembles and starts to rise, when a cry bursts out in the auditorium: "Not yet!"

                                    And

                 THE MANAGER OF THE THEATER
           *springing from his box near the proscenium, jumps down to
             the orchestra. An imposing man wearing a tuxedo, he runs
                          toward the stage, repeating:*

Not yet!

              *The curtain falls back. The Manager leans for a moment
              against the proscenium and then begins to speak in verse:*

             The curtain is a wall that flies.
And when it's curtain time, one shouldn't wait
Impatiently and chafe for the wall to rise;
A wall is a charming thing to contemplate.

It's charming to sit before a great red wall
That hangs in silent, velvety suspense;
Ah—then the curtain throbs, and best of all,
Behind it you can hear the sounds commence.

Tonight, please give your imagination rein;
Dream, and listen to all the sounds; and let
Them set the scene.

> *The Manager bends to hear the sounds that*
> *begin to come from the stage.*
>   A step... is there a lane?
> Wings... a garden?
> *As the curtain throbs, he cries precipitately:*
>   No, don't raise it yet!
> *Bending again to listen, he notes the sounds,*
> *vague or precise, mingled or distinct, that will*
> *come from behind the curtain from now on.*

A soaring magpie calls a piercing sally;
Boots on flagstones run fortissimo;
It must be a yard... that overlooks a valley:
Shouts and songs and barking drift from below.

Bit by bit the scene will crystallize.
Sound will paint the scenery around us.
A bell is tinkling faintly; now it dies.
A goat—there must be greenery around us.

High above us there must be a tree
Because a finch pours song from a golden throat.
And since a voice is raised in mimicry,
There must be a cage and a bird who sings by rote.

Water drums in a pail and overflows...
A barrow clatters, pushed by a steady arm,
A roof with pigeons plays at tic-tac-toes...
Yes, our ears are sketching in a farm.

The rustle of straw, the swish of tails and tether:
Surely there's a barn or a loft of hay.
Church bells: Sunday. Cicadas: sunny weather.
Jays: the forest can't be far away.

Sssh! Nature is dreaming, modulating
The day's rich clangor into strange new keys,
Composing an overture, and orchestrating
It by the night, the distance, and the whisper of a breeze.

A tractor rolls to a stop. A gate is barred.
A truck starts up. A window creaks and descends.
Can't you see it now—the old farmyard?
The dog who sleeps and the cat who just pretends.

It's Sunday. The farmers are going to leave for the fair.
                    A ROUGH VOICE, *behind the curtain*
Come on, come on!

AN IMPATIENT VOICE
Aren't you ready, Joe?
We won't be back till late tonight.
A GIRL'S VOICE

My hair!

ANOTHER VOICE
Close the shutters!

A MAN'S VOICE
Right!
A WOMEN'S VOICE
My purse!
A MAN'S VOICE, *as the truck's engine races*

Let's go!

MANAGER
The truck pulls out, trailing an exhaust
Of songs and laughter... then it fades away;
It's cut in two by a turn in the road... it's lost...
There's no one left. Now we can have the play.

Malebranche would say no souls remain.
With all respect, we think there are still some hearts.
The drama isn't man's exclusive domain.
Without him, joy and grief still play their parts.

He listens again.

A bumblebee, a furry cloud of humming,
Stops... drawn in by a flower's honeyed look.
We can begin. Tonight our cues aren't coming
From a prompter's booth, but straight from Aesop's book.

Our characters are small, and so...
calling up into the flies

Eugene!

to the audience
My chief stagehand...
calling again
You can lower it now!
A VOICE, *from the flies*

Will do!

MANAGER
We're letting down a large invisible screen
Of special glass, to magnify the view.
He listens again.

The Stradivari lift their crystal bows;
They're tuning up already here in the blue.
Sssh! It's time for the lobby doors to close
Because the little crickets are taking their cue

From a brown conductor wearing a glossy coat.
Frrrt! The bee comes out, with powdered wings.
A hen appears, just as La Fontaine wrote.
And just as in Beethoven, a cuckoo sings.

And now, because we'll see through Nature's eyes
And cuckoos will direct our poetic flights...
Sssh! The time has come for the curtain to rise:
The firefly crew is turning out the lights.

The curtain rises.

ACT ONE

The Evening
of the Pheasant

THE SCENE: The interior of a farmyard.

The sounds have described it exactly. A tumble-down gate. A low wall overgrown with umbels. Hay. Manure. Piles of straw. And the countryside in the distance.

On the house, a mauve cataract of wistaria. In a corner, the old watchdog's kennel. A cart. A well. Scattered about, all the tools the Earth needs.

Sunshine. Sometimes a wing beats, and then a feather floats for a moment. A warm silence, filled with happy clucking.

AT RISE: ALL THE BARNYARD. HENS, CHICKENS, walking about or climbing and descending the little stair of the henhouse. CHICKS, DUCKS, TURKEYS, etc. THE BLACKBIRD in his cage, which hangs among the wistaria; THE CAT sleeping on the wall; A BUTTERFLY poised among the flowers.

WHITE HEN, *pecking*

Delicious!

ANOTHER HEN, *running*
What're you chewing?

ALL THE HENS, *running*
What's she chewing?

WHITE HEN

The little bug they call the tiger beetle,
Who gives the beak a scent of jasmine and rose.

BLACK HEN
stopped before the Blackbird's cage, listening

The Blackbird's so artistic. Yes, he whistles
Just as if he were —

WHITE HEN
A city bird.

TURKEY, *solemnly correcting*

Who takes his art from nature.

DUCK
Still, he never

Ends his song.

TURKEY
To end it, that would be
Too easy.
He sings the air the Blackbird whistles:
"I long to reap. . . to reap. . . to reap. . ."
True art cannot have limits placed upon it.
"To reap. . . to reap. . . " Bravo!

The Blackbird comes out on a wistaria branch and bows.

A CHICK, *astonished*
Can he come out?

BLACKBIRD, *bowing*
Yes, when the public clamors, I appear.

He goes back in.

CHICK
But what about his cage?

TURKEY
The door is made
Without a spring; he's free to come and go.
"To reap. . . to reap. . . " How superficial, if
He were to name the thing he's reaping.

BLACK HEN
seeing the Butterfly poised on the flowers
that hang over the wall at the rear
Oh!
The gorgeous Butterfly!

WHITE HEN
Oh, where?

BLACK HEN
He's on
The honeysuckle.

TURKEY, *pedantically*
That butterfly is called
A Monarch.

CHICK, *eyes on the Butterfly*
Now he's on the pink!

WHITE HEN, *to the Turkey*
A Monarch?
Why?

BLACKBIRD, *poking his head through the bars*
Because it's hard to pin him down.

WHITE HEN
The Blackbird... he's a scream!

TURKEY, *shaking his head*
He's more than that.

ANOTHER HEN
A butterfly is chic.

BLACKBIRD
But very easy
To make: You put a W on top
Of a Y.

A HEN
With four quick strokes of his beak, he draws
A caricature!

TURKEY
Not just a caricature,
An insight. Hen, this Blackbird wants to reach
The mind as well as hit the funny-bone.
He teaches while he wears a clown's disguise.

A CHICK, *to a chicken*
Mama, why does the Cat despise the Dog?

BLACKBIRD, *sticking out his head*
Because he takes her theater seat.

CHICK
They have
A theater?

BLACKBIRD
Yes, for fairy tales.

CHICK
But where?

BLACKBIRD
The hearth, you see, where both of them would like
To watch the Sleeping-Beauty-Log start blushing
When she wakes up next to Prince Charcoal.

TURKEY, *dazzled by this so-called wit*
How shrewdly he reveals the hatred of races
As, in essence, just a fight for places.
Marvellous!

BEIGE HEN, *to the White Hen, who is pecking*
You eat those peppers?

WHITE HEN

Often.

BEIGE HEN

Why?

WHITE HEN
They make the feathers rosy.

BEIGE HEN

Oh?

A DISTANT VOICE

Cuckoo!

WHITE HEN

Listen.

THE VOICE
Cuckoo!

WHITE HEN

There's the Cuckoo.

A GRAY HEN, *running up, feverishly*
Oh, which one? From the woods, or the one in the clock?

THE VOICE, MORE DISTANT

Cuckoo!

WHITE HEN

The woods.

GRAY HEN
Oh, good. I thought I'd missed

The other one.

WHITE HEN, *going to her*
It's true you love him, then?

> GRAY HEN, *sadly*
But sight unseen. He lives in the kitchen, high
In a chalet hung above the gun and the coat.
As soon as he sings, I run... but the moment I
Get there, his little wicket closes. So,
Tonight I'll stay on the sill.

> *She stations herself by the door.*

> A VOICE
> White Hen!

> WHITE HEN, *looking around with jerks of her head*
> Who calls?

> THE VOICE
A pigeon!

> WHITE HEN
Where?

> PIGEON
> On the sloping roof!

> WHITE HEN, *lifting her head and seeing him*
> Ah, yes.

> PIGEON
Although I've got an urgent letter, still
I'm stopping. Hello, Hen.

> WHITE HEN
> Hello, mailman.

> PIGEON
This summer night, my work in the Airmail Service
Takes me through your skies, and I would be
So thrilled if I could only...

> WHITE HEN, *spying a kernel*
> Just a minute.

> ANOTHER HEN, *running to her with curiosity*
What're you chewing?

> ALL THE HENS, *running*
> What's she chewing?

> WHITE HEN
> Wheat.

GRAY HEN, *continuing, to the White Hen*
Tonight I'll stay on the sill.

She indicates the door of the house.

WHITE HEN
The door is shut.

GRAY HEN
I know, but when it strikes the hour, I'll stretch
My neck and view the Cuckoo through...

PIGEON, *impatiently*
White Hen!

WHITE HEN
One minute.
to the Gray Hen
View the Cuckoo through?

GRAY HEN
indicating the round hole near the bottom of the door
The cat-hole.

PIGEON
You leave me here with my beak wide open! Hey!
Whitest of hens!

WHITE HEN, *hopping toward him*
Now, you were saying what?

PIGEON
That I would be...

WHITE HEN
Be what, bluest of pigeons?

PIGEON
Thrilled if I... oh no, it's much too bold...
If I could see...

WHITE HEN
See what?

PIGEON, *emotionally*
For just a moment...

ALL THE HENS, *impatiently*
What?

PIGEON

His crest.

WHITE HEN, *to the others, laughing*
Oh my, he wants to see...

PIGEON, *very excited*

Yes, yes, I want to see...

WHITE HEN
Calm down.

PIGEON

I'm stamping

With excitement.

WHITE HEN
Don't go through the roof.

PIGEON

But we admire him.

WHITE HEN
So does everyone.

PIGEON

I told my wife I'd find out what he's like.

WHITE HEN, *pecking all the while*

Superb, one can't deny.

PIGEON

From where we live
We hear him sing. He is The One whose song
Sheds greater light on the countryside than a village
Casts on its mountain-slope, because his voice
Is always there, a shimmer hung in the distance;
He is The One whose crowing pierces the blue
Horizon like a needle threaded with gold
That stitches the tops of the hills to the hem of the sky.
He is The Cock!

BLACKBIRD, *pacing in his cage*
For whom all hearts go tick-tock.

TURKEY

Soon he will return from his rounds in the fields.

PIGEON

Ah, sir! You know him, then?

TURKEY, *importantly*

I saw his birth.

This chick — to me he'll always be a chick —
Was sent to me to take his bugle lessons.

PIGEON

Ah, you teach...

TURKEY

I certainly can tutor

Cock-a-doodle-dooing: I'm a gobbler.

PIGEON, *avidly*

Where was he born?

TURKEY
indicating an old covered basket, worn and full of holes

In that old basket, there.

PIGEON

The hen who brooded him, is she alive?

TURKEY

Oh, yes. She's there.

PIGEON
Where?

TURKEY

In that old basket.

PIGEON, *more and more interested*

What's her breed?

TURKEY

Traditional. She's just

A good old-fashioned hen, born in the South.

BLACKBIRD, *sticking out his head*

The one they wanted to put in every pot.

PIGEON

To brood the Cock... she must be very proud.

TURKEY

Yes, with a humble foster-mother's pride.
Her chick — and this is all she comprehends —

Is growing. When you tell her that, her clouded
Reason gives a momentary spark.
> *He shouts to the basket:*
Hey there, old one! He's growing!

ALL THE HENS
Growing!

> *Immediately the lid of the basket lifts*
> *and an old ruffled head rises into view.*

PIGEON, *to the Old Hen, with feeling*
Hey,

Old one, do you like to hear he's growing?

OLD HEN, *nodding her head, sententiously*
Sure.
> *Wednesday's wheat redounds to Tuesday's credit.*

> *She disappears. The lid falls back.*

TURKEY
Now and then she lifts the lid, and crack!
Before it falls, she drops a pearl of old
Folk-wisdom, a proverb she made up herself. . .

PIGEON
White Hen!

TURKEY, *moving away*
. . .one that sometimes finds its mark.

OLD HEN, *reappearing behind him*
> *When the peacock's gone, the turkey spreads his tail.*

> *The Turkey swings around; the lid has fallen.*

PIGEON, *to the White Hen*
Is it true that Chantecler is never hoarse?

WHITE HEN, *continually pecking*
It's true.

PIGEON
You must be very proud that here,
Beneath these elms, you have a Cock whose name
Will join the ranks of Famous Animals
And live for decades.

TURKEY
Very proud.

to a Chick

Who are

The Famous Animals?

CHICK, *reciting*

Noah's Dove,

Saint Roch's Poodle, the Horse of Cali...

TURKEY

Cali...?

CHICK

Cali...

PIGEON
They say his song is bold and bright
And strong enough to lighten work and frighten
Away the birds of prey; is it true?

WHITE HEN

It's true.

CHICK

Cali... Cali...

PIGEON
White Hen, is it really true
That his song protects the warm and sacred egg
And keeps the weasel from oozing into the coop
And staining the front of his shirt...

BLACKBIRD, *sticking out his head*

With egg-drop soup?

WHITE HEN

It's true.

CHICK

Cali...

TURKEY
Gu...

CHICK
Gu...

PIGEON

White Hen, is it true. . .

CHICK, *leaping with joy at remembering*

Gula!

PIGEON
. . .what they say: that he must have a secret,
One that gives such ringing brass to his crow
That it makes the trumpet-flowers try to blow?

WHITE HEN, *a bit wearied by the questions*

It's true.

PIGEON
And no one knows the secret?

WHITE HEN

No.

PIGEON

He hasn't even told his hen?

WHITE HEN, *correcting him*

His hens!

PIGEON, *a bit shocked*
You mean that he has more than one?

BLACKBIRD

He sings!

But you just bill and coo.

PIGEON

He hasn't told

His favorite hen?

TUFTED HEN, *quickly*
Oh, no.

WHITE HEN, *just as quickly*
Oh, no.

BLACK HEN, *the same*

Oh, no.

BLACKBIRD, *sticking out his head*
Be quiet! Watch the tragedy unfold.
Our tiny Pegasus who paws the air
Is unaware. . .

*A large green net appears above the wall and gently approaches
the Butterfly, who has settled on one of the flowers.*

A HEN
What's that?

TURKEY, *solemnly*
It's Fate.

BLACKBIRD

In gauze.

WHITE HEN
Oh, dear... a bamboo pole with a nasty net.

BLACKBIRD
And on the other end is a nasty brat.
in a low voice, watching the Butterfly
You fashion-plate who sails where the breezes take you,
Soon you'll be as neat as a pin can make you.

EVERYONE
watching the net slowly approach over the wall
Closer... Yes... It's coming... Inch by inch...
He's caught! — He's not!

The Butterfly is about to be captured. But:

A SUDDEN VOICE IN THE DISTANCE
Cock-a-doodle-doo!

*At the sound the Butterfly flits away.
The Net hovers in disappointment and then disappears.*

SEVERAL HENS
Hey, what was that?

A HEN
who has hopped on a wheelbarrow to watch the Butterfly
He's far above the meadow.

BLACKBIRD, *ironically*
That was Chantecler, in shining armor.

PIGEON
Chantecler!

A HEN
He's coming!

ANOTHER HEN
Almost here!

WHITE HEN, *to the Pigeon*
Now you'll see a handsome rooster.

BLACKBIRD

An easy
Thing to make.

TURKEY
He always has an answer.

BLACKBIRD
Take a juicy melon, that's the trunk.
For legs, two stalks of asparagus. The head,
A ripe pimento. Eyes, two beady currants.
Make the tail with a scallion trailing blue
And green. For ears, a pair of kidney beans.
And there it is. A Cock!

PIGEON, *gently*
Without a crow.

BLACKBIRD, *pointing to Chantecler, who appears on the wall*
A mere detail. Don't you see the likeness?

PIGEON
Not at all!
looking at Chantecler with very different eyes
Beneath that crest I see
The splendid Knight of Summer drawing near,
Who drapes himself in gold by borrowing
His cape from wagons shimmering with wheat,
And sweeps it up behind him with a sickle!

CHANTECLER, *on the wall, in a long, guttural sigh*
Co-o-o-o-ck...

BLACKBIRD
When he makes that noise and starts to strut
He's either got a song in mind... or a hen.

CHANTECLER, *motionless on the wall, head high*
Kindle! Glow!

BLACKBIRD
Sounds like hot air.

CHANTECLER

Inflame!

A HEN

Look — he stops, with a lifted claw. . .

CHANTECLER, *in a kind of rattle of tenderness*

Co-o-o-o-ck. . .

BLACKBIRD

Now that, that's ecstasy.

CHANTECLER

The only gold

With wisdom comes from you. I worship you!

PIGEON, *softly*

Whom can he be talking to?

BLACKBIRD, *banteringly*

The sun.

CHANTECLER

You dry the tears of the tiniest weed with ease,
You bring dead flowers to life in the butterfly;
You warm the wind that cajoles the cherry trees
          To shed their blooms, like destinies,
          So they may grow and multiply.

I worship you, o Sun! whose aureole,
To bless each brow and turn all nectar sweet,
Surrounds each cottage and fills each flower's bowl;
          You divide yourself but are always whole;
          Like mother-love, you stay replete.

I sing of you; take me as priest of your mass,
You who use soap bubbles as a place to dwell,
And often choose, when you sink below the grass,
          To let the humble window-glass
          Hold the torch of your last farewell.

BLACKBIRD, *poking his head through the bars*

We'll never stop him, children: it's an ode.

TURKEY

*watching Chantecler, who comes down from the wall
on the steps of a pile of hay*

He's coming, prouder. . .

A HEN, *stopping before a little tin cone*
Look! a trough!
She drinks.

How handy!

BLACKBIRD
...Prouder than a patriot waving a flag!

CHANTECLER, *beginning to walk about the yard*
You make the sunflower...

ALL THE HENS, *running to the White Hen*
What's she chewing?

WHITE HEN

Corn.

CHANTECLER
You make the sunflower lift her head to explore,
You burnish my brother-of-gold on the weather-vane,
You steal through the trees, and down through the leaves you pour
A shifting, drifting golden floor
Whose beauty footsteps would profane.

You glaze the pottery jug with a single stroke,
You make a flying flag of a drying towel,
The haystack, thanks to you, wears a golden cloak,
And her little sister, the beehive, woke
This morning wearing a golden cowl.

Glory to you on the fields! Upon all the vines!
From the tops of the hills to the valley, your blessing prevails!
On the wing of the swan, in the eye of the lizard it shines!
O you who draw the broad outlines
And render in the last details!

For all you touch you cut out a darker twin
Who stretches and goes to bed at her sister's feet;
You double the number of things we can revel in,
For each has a shadow next-of-kin
Who's often lovelier to meet.

You fill the air with scent, the stream with fire.
You make the bush a place where a god may light.
You turn the gloomy tree to a sacred choir.
Without you things could not aspire
Past what they are, to what they might!

PIGEON

Bravo! I'll tell my wife of this for years!

CHANTECLER

Young blue stranger who has a greenhorn beak,
I thank you. Lay my respects at her coral feet.

The Pigeon flies off.

BLACKBIRD

He has to look after his fan club.

CHANTECLER, *cordially, to all*

Everyone,

Let's get to work! And let's enjoy the work
We do. — Ganders! Gentlemen, it's time
To take your geese to the pond.

A GANDER, *nonchalantly*

Oh, really?

CHANTECLER, *marching on him*

Now then,

No more idle hissing and honking!

The Ganders leave quickly.

You,

Old Hen, before tonight, you have to pick off
Thirty-two slugs, at least. — Future Cock,
Go practice, sing your cock-a-doodle-doo
Four hundred times before the echo.

COCKEREL, *a bit put out*

The echo?

CHANTECLER

That is how I limbered up my glottis
When I still needed to wear the egg-shell diaper.

A HEN, *pretentiously*

None of that is very interesting.

CHANTECLER

Everything is interesting! Please
Go brood the eggs that you were given.

The Hen leaves quickly. To another:

You,

Go check the verbena. Gulp down everything
That's chewing on it. Oh, if the caterpillar

Thinks we'll make her a gift of our flowers, she
Can just... turn over a whole new leaf.
                          The Hen leaves. To another:
                                                        You,
Go stop the grasshoppers' siege of the cabbage patch.
You —
                    *He spots the Old Hen, whose head has
                    just lifted the lid of the basket.*
          Well, hello, nursey.
                        She looks at him admiringly.
                                    Have I grown?

OLD HEN
Sooner or later the frog must emerge from the tadpole.

CHANTECLER
Yes.
          The lid falls back. To the Hens, resuming his commanding tone
                          Line up, now! Off to peck
In the meadows, stepping lively!

          WHITE HEN, *to the Gray Hen*
                                    Aren't you coming?

GRAY HEN
Sssh! I'm staying here, to see the Cuckoo.

CHANTECLER
Speckled Hen, you seem a little sulky.

          SPECKLED HEN, *going to him*
Cock...

CHANTECLER
          What is it?

SPECKLED HEN
          I'm the one you prefer...

CHANTECLER
Sssh!

SPECKLED HEN
          And so it hurts me not to know...

          WHITE HEN, *approaching him from the other side*
Cock...

CHANTECLER
What is it?

WHITE HEN, *coaxing*
I'm your favorite hen...

CHANTECLER
Sssh!

WHITE HEN
And so I would like to know...

BLACK HEN, *approaching softly*
Cock...

CHANTECLER
What is it?

BLACK HEN
I'm your special pet.

CHANTECLER
Sssh!

BLACK HEN
So tell it to me...

WHITE HEN
...The secret, please...

SPECKLED HEN
...Of your song?
She moves closer, and in a voice filled with curiosity
I think you have a little copper thing
Inside your trachea.

CHANTECLER
Yes, it's hidden well.

WHITE HEN, *same business*
Perhaps you do what all great tenors do,
Eat raw eggs.

CHANTECLER
Ugh! a Thyestian banquet?

BLACK HEN, *same business*
Maybe this is it: You make a special
Mud-pack...

CHANTECLER
To catch the frogs in my throat? That's it.

ALL THREE

Cock...

CHANTECLER, *brusquely*
Go!
All the Hens start to leave; he calls them back.
While your blood-red combs are rising and falling
In and out of sight among the borders,
Just like poppies playing hide-and-seek,
Be certain you don't hurt the real poppies.
Ladies are sometimes careless where they walk
Not knowing it's a crime to crush a flower,
Even with a woman: You, my hens,
Be full of loving care for all those blooms
Whose only crime is pushing up through the field.
The wildest flower has the right to beauty.
If an insect, red and stippled black,
Walks out upon a path of Queen Anne's Lace,
Pluck off the walker, but don't hurt the walk!
It seems to me the flowers of the field are sisters
Who all should fall beneath the plow together.
Go!
They start to leave. He calls them back.
Remember, when hens go...

A HEN, *bowing*

To the field...

CHANTECLER

The leader...

ALL THE HENS, *bowing*

Leads.

CHANTECLER
Now go.
They start to leave. He calls them back.
A word or two.
Never stop to peck while crossing the road.
The Hens bow.
Now you may cross.

A HORN, *in the distance*
Honk! Honk! Honk!

CHANTECLER
rushing in front of them, wings spread

Not yet!

THE HORN
very near, accompanied by a horrible roaring
Honk! Honk! Honk!

CHANTECLER
barring the way, while all the Hens tremble

Wait!

THE HORN, *far away*

Honk! Honk! Honk!

CHANTECLER, *letting them pass*

Now you can go.

GRAY HEN

No one could see me.

SPECKLED HEN, *last to leave*
How amusing! Everything

We eat will taste of gasoline.

CHANTECLER, *to himself after a pause*
No, I cannot let a frivolous soul
Share a secret whose glory weighs like stone.
Forget it!
shaking his feathers
Let's rejoice in being the Cock!

He prances up and down.
I'm handsome. Proud. I leap. I dart.
I stop or I sketch out a *grand jeté.*
And sometimes with an affair of the heart
I scandalize the cart
Till it throws up its shafts to pray!

Trouble can wait! Being happy is better!
Let's chew grain! My head and throat,
When I lift them high, wear something redder
Than a robin has for sweater
Or a cardinal has for a coat!

It's warm. All's well. I strut. I skip.
My duty done, I stroll here and there,

As the Blackbird says, on an ego trip,
        And like d'Artagnan, slip. . .

A VOICE, *terrible*

Chantecler, beware!

CHANTECLER

Who's telling me to beware?

There is a rustling of straw in the dog's corner.

PATOU, *barking from his corner*
Me! Me!

       He appears.

CHANTECLER

Patou, is that you, a good old tousled head
Coming out of the dark with straw in your eyes?

PATOU

Yes!

To see the blinders over yourrrrs!

CHANTECLER

You're angry?

PATOU

Rrrr. . .

CHANTECLER

When he rolls his r's, he's really mad.

PATOU

It's love of you that makes me roll my rrrr's. . .
I guard the house, the field, and the garden; what
I must protect above all else is your song.
And so I growl at danger. That's my nature.

CHANTECLER

Hot under the collar?

PATOU

Making jokes? That's bad!

Psychologist that I am, I know there's danger.
    He sniffs.
The terrier in me can smell a rat.

CHANTECLER

You're not a terrier.

> PATOU, *shaking his head*
>>> Chantecler,

How do we know?

> CHANTECLER, *studying him*
>> It's true your breed is odd.

What are you, actually?

> PATOU
>>>> A dreadful mixture.

I'm the son of every passer-by.
Inside me yaps the voice of every blood:
Mastiffs, beagles, pointers, poodles, hounds.
My soul is a pack, a whole round table, brooding.
I'm every dog there is, I've been them all.

> CHANTECLER

There must be a lot of goodness in you, then.

> PATOU

We're brothers, made to understand each other!
You sing songs to the sun and scratch in the earth:
I, when I want to give myself a treat...

> CHANTECLER

You lie on the earth and sleep in the sun!

> PATOU, *with a happy little yap*
>>>> Yes!

> CHANTECLER

This double love will always bind us together.

> PATOU

I love the sun so much that I howl at the moon;
I adore the earth to such a point that I'm always
Digging holes to put my nose inside.

> CHANTECLER

The gardener's wife knows all about it! But where
Do you see danger? All is calm and bright.
My humble, golden realm does not seem threatened.

> OLD HEN
> *her head coming out of the basket*
> *The egg looks just like marble until it breaks!*

> CHANTECLER, *to Patou*

What kind of danger?

PATOU
Two. First, in that cage...

The Blackbird is heard whistling.

CHANTECLER

Well?

PATOU

That whistler.

CHANTECLER
What does he do?

PATOU

Spread chaos!

CHANTECLER

What?

PATOU

All over!

CHANTECLER, *ironic*
Oh, the devil!

PEACOCK, *crying, in the distance*

Eee...yong!

PATOU

And then that cry...

PEACOCK, *farther away*
Eee...yong!

PATOU

More out of tune
All by itself than a whole church choir.

CHANTECLER

A whistler,
Then, and a poser. But what have they done to you?

PATOU
They've made me sure they'll do some things to you!
Here, where the animals are pure and good,
The Peacock puts on airs and the Blackbird scoffs.
One has the false and grotesque manners which
He learned parading the lawns of the super-rich;
The other has his slang and his cynical air

That he must have picked up while he was who knows where;
One is a travelling salesman for acid laughter,
The other a witless ambassador of Fashion;
Each a saboteur of love and work,
One by taunting, the other by flaunting his tail.
Those two have brought us, here in our golden light,
The two worst plagues in the world, the saddest blight:
The word that always wants to be know as wit,
The style that always wants to be known as "it"!
It's wheat, not chaff, that you have always preferred,
So how can you be friends with that...wretched bird?

> *The Blackbird is heard practicing, whistling*
> *"I long to reap... to reap... to reap..."*

A bird who makes hard work of a song!

CHANTECLER, *indulgently*

He whistles

It, that's all.

PATOU
grudgingly, in a little attenuated growl
Ye-e-e-s. But not to the end.

CHANTECLER, *watching the Blackbird hop*
He's light of heart.

PATOU, *same business*
Ye-e-e-s. But how he weighs
On our souls. A bird who agrees to use a trapeze!

CHANTECLER
And then, you must admit he's smart.

PATOU
whose growl grows longer and longer

Ye-e-e-e-s.

But not so very, because his eyes never shine.
He stands in front of a flower and looks at the stem!
He always deprecates and qualifies.

CHANTECLER
But he has taste.

PATOU
Ye-e-e-s. But not very much.
Wearing black is the easiest kind of taste.
You have to risk your colors on your wing.

CHANTECLER
Of course, he has an individual style.
He's quite amusing.

PATOU
Ye-e-e—no! Amusing,
To use catch-phrases and pass them off as wit?

CHANTECLER
He has a gift for the unexpected.

PATOU
                                                            Quick,
But crude. I don't think it's verbal magic
To look at a grazing cow and say: "I hope
She's got the stomachs for that." And I doubt that it takes
A special genius to tell the duck: "You're a quack."
No, I detest the Blackbird's brand of humor:
It's as devoid of wit as it is of style.

CHANTECLER
It's not entirely his fault; he wears
The latest fashion.

PATOU
Oh?

CHANTECLER
                                        In that well-cut
Tuxedo, he looks—

PATOU
                    Just like an undertaker
Dancing with joy because he's buried Faith.

CHANTECLER, *laughing*
Come on, you paint him blacker than he is.

PATOU
I think a Blackbird is just a crow who failed.

CHANTECLER
He's not big enough for that.

PATOU
shaking his ears with a vengeance
                                Don't let that fool you!
Evil starts by making small-scale models.
Don't assume they're good because they're small.

The soul of a bayonet is in the pen-knife;
Crow and Blackbird come from the same piece of crepe,
And the black and yellow wasp contains the tiger.

                    CHANTECLER, *amused by Patou's fury*
So, the Blackbird is wicked, stupid, ugly...

                              PATOU
The main thing is... that you can't tell what he is!
Does he ever think? Or feel? "Tew-tew-tew!"

                         CHANTECLER
But what harm does he do?

                              PATOU
                                        He tew-tew-tews!
And nothing could be more lethal to feeling and thought
Than a tew-tew-tew that's full of sound, but empty.
Every day—that's why I roll my r's—
I see the debasing of hearts and vocabularies.
Oh, it's enough to drive a dog mad!

                         CHANTECLER
                                          But Patou...

                              PATOU
He thinks that everything should be a joke.
Now, we all know I have no pedigrees,
But he's always saying to me: "Your papers, please?"
Oh, to escape, to follow a beggar, even,
But at least, when you drink from a pond at night,
To have what's better than any marrow bone:
The sweet illusion of lapping up the stars!

                         CHANTECLER
          amazed that on these last words Patou lowered his voice
Why do you lower your voice?

                              PATOU
                                        Today, you see,
That's what we have to do when we speak of the stars.
          Sadly he puts his head on his paws.

                    CHANTECLER, *consoling him*
Now, now.

                    PATOU, *standing up again*
          It's weak and stupid, that's what it is.
I'll shout it out if I want to.

> *howling with all his might*
> Stars!
>> *then, in relief*
>> Thank heavens.

SOME PULLETS
passing through at the rear, snickering
Stars! —My stars, he's seeing stars!

They leave, clowning.

PATOU
                                                                            Hear that?
Next thing you know, our pullets will learn to whistle.

CHANTECLER
What do I care? I sing! and the hens are all
With me.

PATOU
Don't count on the heart of a hen—or a crowd.
Beak-service, that is all you get from them.

CHANTECLER
But love is tribute paid in little kisses.

PATOU
I was young once, too. I had a raving
Beauty... big hot eyes, and the rest to match.
Well, I was deceived. For someone better-looking?
No! for a mutt!
suddenly bellowing
                    Deceived for what? for what?
Do you know?

CHANTECLER, *backing away*
You scare me.

PATOU
A basset who walked on his ears!

BLACKBIRD
who has heard Patou's last shouts, pokes his head through the bars
Oh, no! Is he still harping about that basset?
What about it? You were two-timed. So?
So were we all. A trifling incident.
Even I, as clever as I am,
I'm just another cuckold—dressed in black
And trying to pass it off as widower's weeds.

PATOU
A joke like that from you is a bit of a puzzle.
Still, there are certain subjects we should—

BLACKBIRD
Muzzle!

PATOU
Just what are you, scofffing at everything
Up there?

BLACKBIRD
The mocking-bird of the poultry yard.

PATOU
Bad luck, that's what you'll bring.

BLACKBIRD
You're telling fortunes?
I'll come down.
*He comes out of his cage, hopping down
the length of the twisted wistaria branches.*
Good old wistaria...
It's always hanging around...

PATOU
Rrrr...

CHANTECLER
Sssh!
He is a friend.

PATOU
Just don't turn your back.

CHANTECLER, *to the Blackbird*
Fine things I hear when they start to talk about you.

OLD HEN, *head emerging from the basket*
*He who moves a rotten log will see
The wood-lice run.*

The lid falls back.

PATOU, *to Chantecler*
He jokes about you, you know.

BLACKBIRD
So, retriever, now you're carrying tales?

PATOU
When you're exhausting your heart in a fervent song,
He says it puts the teeth of your comb on edge.

CHANTECLER, *to the Blackbird*
Do you say that?

BLACKBIRD, *ingenuously*
Do you mind? It can't hurt you,
And a joke on you is always good for a laugh.

PATOU
See here, do you admire the Cock, or scoff?

BLACKBIRD
I laugh at the parts but admire the whole.

PATOU
You always
Peck two kinds of seed.

BLACKBIRD, *pointing to his cage*
I've got two seed-cups.

PATOU
I come straight to the point.

BLACKBIRD
And beat it to death.
You're just an old retired army dog.
Now I am a bird who's up to date.

PATOU
sharply, rushing at him but held back by his chain
On what?
Move! or that nice black rump will have a red stump!
The Blackbird moves away quickly.
Patou goes back to his corner, muttering:
There, now he's up to date on something.

CHANTECLER
Calm down!
It's just his way. In fact, if this Blackbird
Were placed before a sight of real beauty,
He would applaud.

PATOU
But only with one wing.
What else could you expect from a bird who leaves

His cage, who sees the woods and the sweet woodbine,
And goes back in to eat a dry old biscuit?

                        BLACKBIRD
Never once does it seem to cross his mind
That the poacher's hands aren't always lily-white.

                        PATOU
I know that the underbrush is filled with gold!

                        BLACKBIRD
But sometimes that which glitters is made of lead.
They're all out hunting for pot-pies up in the skies;
They'll pop pie-crust on anything that flies,
Including four and twenty— Hey, what a blow
If a pot-shot laid me low and I baked in dough!

                        PATOU
Does the great stag find his forest less superb
Because his hoof can strike on a rusting cartridge?

                        BLACKBIRD
No, old boy... but then, the stag has a hatrack
Where his brains should be.

                        PATOU
                                        Oh! ...but freedom,
Under the eyes of the violets! And love!

                        BLACKBIRD
Those games you play in the boondocks—spare me, please.
Not one of them is worth my new trapeze.
Oh, my cage! Let's sign a three-year lease.
You live like a king, there's filtered water to drink...
          Patou makes a move toward him; he clears away, adding
Sling mud, who cares? I've got a private bath.

                        CHANTECLER, *a bit impatient*
Why do you always stoop to playing the clown?

                        BLACKBIRD
Because it's amusing, putting everything down.

                        PATOU
Rrrr....

                        CHANTECLER
Amusing? Where did you learn that?

BLACKBIRD
From a city sparrow. That's the way it's done
In town.

CHANTECLER
I knew a robin who had lived
In a city park for years. I never heard
Him talk that way.

BLACKBIRD
Well, what do you want from me?
I'm just a child of the times. Today no beak
Is really chic unless it has some sting.

PATOU
There they are, those words that make me fume!
This clown with his "sting," the Peacock with his "chic."

CHANTECLER, *disdainfully*
Oh, the Peacock.

PATOU, *furious*
Yes, the Peacock!

BLACKBIRD, *pointing to Patou's muzzle*
Look,
He's all in a lather.

CHANTECLER
What is the Peacock up to?

BLACKBIRD
Making eyes with his tail.

PATOU
And influencing
Simpler hearts with his airs and his strutting about.

CHANTECLER
But where do you see any signs of that?

PATOU
In a thousand little nothings.

OLD HEN, *appearing*
Soapy bubbles
Downstream tell of washerwomen upstream.

The lid falls back.

                              CHANTECLER
I have never seen the smallest bubble...

                                PATOU
                    pointing to a Guinea Pig passing through
There, that Guinea Pig.

                              CHANTECLER
                                          The yellow fellow?

                        GUINEA PIG, *annoyed, correcting him*
Khaki.

                          CHANTECLER, *to Patou*
            Kha...?

                                PATOU
                              A bubble.
                                pointing to a Duck passing through
                                    And then that duck...

              CHANTECLER, *looking at the Duck, laughing*
He's on his way to his bath.

                    DUCK, *turning and dryly correcting him*
                                        My sauna.

                        CHANTECLER, *astonished*
                                                    Sau...?

                                PATOU
A bubble.

                        Within the house is heard
                      THE CUCKOO IN THE CLOCK
                  Cuckoo!

                              GRAY HEN
        leaving her hiding-place and running distractedly to the cat-hole
                          He! It's he! At last
I'm going to see him!
                    She sticks her head in the hole.
                    The cuckoo has stopped.
                          No, too late!
                                    shouting
                                          Encore!

                    CHANTECLER, *turning around*
What?

GRAY HEN, *desperate, in the cat-hole*
He's stopped!

BLACKBIRD
The half-hour, that's all it was.

CHANTECLER
brusquely, coming up behind the Gray Hen
You're not in the fields?

GRAY HEN, *turning*
Oh, Lord.

CHANTECLER
And why are we

In the cat-hole, sweetheart?

GRAY HEN
Oh, just stretching my neck. . .

CHANTECLER

To see?

GRAY HEN

Oh!

CHANTECLER, *dramatically*
Whom?

GRAY HEN
Oh!

CHANTECLER

Confess!

GRAY HEN, *in the voice of a guilty woman*
The Cuckoo.

CHANTECLER, *amazed*
You love him? Why?

GRAY HEN, *lowering her eyes, with emotion*
He's Swiss.

PATOU

A bubble.

GRAY HEN

He's a thinker.

CHANTECLER
She's in love with a clock!

GRAY HEN
He always appears at the same hour, just like Kant.

CHANTECLER
Like what?

GRAY HEN
Like Kant.

CHANTECLER
I can't believe it. Go!
Get out of my sight!

BLACKBIRD
He's Kanned you, Kant you see?

The Hen dashes off.

CHANTECLER, *pacing in agitation*
Now where did she learn about Kant?

BLACKBIRD
At the Guinea Hen's.

CHANTECLER
That rattle-brained old fool with the painted beak...

PATOU
Is holding a gathering every week.

CHANTECLER
Of grain?

PATOU
Oh, no. Of society.

CHANTECLER
Soci—but where
Do they gather?

BLACKBIRD
Off in a corner of the vegetable garden.

PATOU
Under the tutelage of the old straw man
Whose black silk hat turns greener every day.

CHANTECLER

The scarecrow?

BLACKBIRD
Yes. He gives it more *cachet.*

CHANTECLER

What?

BLACKBIRD
He scares the common birds away.
You can't have poor relations at a soiree.

PATOU, *phlegmatically*

A bubble.

CHANTECLER
A balloon!

BLACKBIRD, *imitating the Guinea Pig*
On Mondays...

CHANTECLER
What do they do

At that old fool's?

PATOU
They cackle and social-climb.
The Pullets push and the Ducklings shove.

BLACKBIRD, *still imitating*

From five

To six...

CHANTECLER
At night?

PATOU
No, in the morning.

CHANTECLER

What?

BLACKBIRD
They need an hour that's fashionable, you see,
When the garden's also empty. So the soiree
Becomes a matinee.

CHANTECLER
                    That's crazy.

BLACKBIRD
                                        Mad.

PATOU
Well, you can't talk. You go there too.

CHANTECLER
                                        He does?

BLACKBIRD
I do. They all admire me.

PATOU
                    And I'm afraid—

CHANTECLER
What next from that brass collar, another "beware"?

PATOU
...That one of these days some hen will lead you there.

CHANTECLER
Me?

PATOU
          You.

CHANTECLER
Me?

PATOU
                    By the end of the beak.

CHANTECLER, *furious*
Me?

PATOU
          Every time we get a new hen
I see you lose your head all over again.

BLACKBIRD
You start to walk around her...
          He imitates the Cock's walk around a hen.
                              "Yes, it's me...
See, here I am!" And then you go: "Co-o-o-..."

CHANTECLER

An idiot, this bird!

BLACKBIRD, *still imitating*

Your wing hangs down...

Your foot does a dance...

A shot is heard in the distance.

Oh-oh, I don't like that.

PATOU, *quivering, sniffing the air*

Big Jules is poaching.

BLACKBIRD

Dog, does it stir you up?

PATOU, *eyes shining, ears cocked*

Yes... it...

suddenly, mastering himself, in an emotional tone

No!

BLACKBIRD

You're turning soft?

PATOU

But it's so dreadful! Maybe some poor partridge...

BLACKBIRD, *slyly*

Look at that. Old age has given him water
On the brain.

PATOU

In the eyes!

BLACKBIRD

See how rheumatism

Leads to animalitarianism.

PATOU

It's just that there are several dogs in me.
I hear a shot; my spaniel's truffle twitches.
But then my poodle's memory evokes
A bloody wing, the glazing eye of a doe,
The last, soft look of a rabbit who ran so hard...
And what wakes up? My heart of a Saint Bernard.

Another shot.

BLACKBIRD, *hiding behind the basket*

Again!

A GOLDEN PHEASANT flies over the wall
and falls wildly into the yard.

PHEASANT

Hide me!

CHANTECLER
Heavens!

PATOU

A golden pheasant!

PHEASANT, *going to Chantecler*
Isn't this the famous Chantecler?

BLACKBIRD, *behind the basket*
That bird's become a household word.

PHEASANT, *running about*

Please save me,

If you're he.

CHANTECLER
I am. I will.

Another shot.

PHEASANT
starting and leaping on Chantecler

Dear God!

CHANTECLER
This pheasant-cock is nervous.

PHEASANT

I'm worn out...

I ran and ran...

He faints.

BLACKBIRD
Looks like he ran out of steam.

CHANTECLER
supporting the Pheasant with one wing
He's handsome. Look how his collar fans around him...
He runs to the trough.
Water! ...I hope his colors won't wash out...
He splashes him with the other wing.
Water!

PHEASANT, *coming to*
Oh! they're after me, please hide me!

BLACKBIRD
My, just like a thriller.

to the Pheasant
How the devil
Could they miss you?

PHEASANT, *pacing distractedly*
I took them by surprise.
The hunter was after a lark. When I rose up,
He shouted, "Son of a gun!" All he saw
Was a flash of gold. All I saw was a flame.
But the dog is chasing me, a dreadful dog—
Finding himself before Patou, he quickly adds
A pointer.
to Chantecler
Hide me!

CHANTECLER
Where? The problem is
That he's so showy. — Sir... noble stranger... —
Where do you hide a rainbow when there's danger?

PATOU
There, by the beehive, stands my house. Go in!
The Pheasant enters, but his long tail sticks out.
These golden capes are really indiscreet.
The tip sticks out... I'd better have a seat.
He sits on the protruding feathers and pretends to be eating the food in his bowl. BRIFFAUT appears above the wall. Long hanging ears and quivering jowls. Patou speaks to him, trying to sound casual.
Hello.

BRIFFAUT, *sniffing*
Mmm, smells good.

PATOU, *modestly, showing his bowl*
Just vegetable soup.

BRIFFAUT
Say, did you see a pheasant-hen go by?

PATOU
A pheasant-hen?

CHANTECLER, *walking about, with forced gaity*
How fierce is our Briffaut!
With his British air, he's very "tally-ho."

PATOU, *to Briffaut*
No, but I saw a pheasant cock.

BRIFFAUT
That's her!

PATOU
The pheasant-hen is always dull and drab.
This bird was gold, a cock. He went that way.

BRIFFAUT
That's her.

CHANTECLER, *going to him, incredulous*
A pheasant-hen is wearing gold?

BRIFFAUT
You haven't heard what sometimes happens?

CHANTECLER AND PATOU
No.

BLACKBIRD
Don't ask that shaggy dog to tell a story!

BRIFFAUT
Well, sometimes... Of course it's very rare:
My master says he read it in Audubon...
It happens that... Extraordinary thing,
You find it too in grouse... Sometimes it happens...

PATOU, *impatient*
What?

BRIFFAUT
That the pheasant-hen... Ah, my friends...

CHANTECLER, *stamping*
Does what?

BRIFFAUT
Decides the male is too well off.
She sees that when he wears his bright spring coat,
He's handsomer than she—

BLACKBIRD
And it gets her goat.

BRIFFAUT

She ceases laying eggs and hatching. Then,
Nature gives her back her purples and golds,
And off she flies, an Amazon, superb
And free, who'd rather have green, gold, and blue
And all the prism's colors upon her back
Than baby pheasants under a dull gray wing.
Rejecting the virtuous role her sex should play,
She leads a life. . .

He makes a derogatory gesture with his paw.

CHANTECLER, *curtly*
And what do you know about it?

BRIFFAUT, *astonished*

What! are you upset?

PATOU, *aside*
Already?

CHANTECLER

So,

In short, this pheasant-cock your master missed. . .

BRIFFAUT

Was a pheasant-hen!
He stops and sniffs.
Wait, now. . .

PATOU, *quickly showing his bowl*
It's just my chow.

BRIFFAUT

Smells tasty.

CHANTECLER, *aside*
I don't like it when he sniffs.

BRIFFAUT, *starting a story*
Let's say that one fine day. . .

BLACKBIRD
He's off again.

A whistle is heard in the distance.

CHANTECLER

They're calling you.

BRIFFAUT
Damnation! Well, good night.

PATOU

Good night!

CHANTECLER
At last, he's gone.

BLACKBIRD, *calling*
Briffaut!

CHANTECLER

Good Lord!

BLACKBIRD, *calling*
There's something I should tell you.

BRIFFAUT
his head reappearing above the wall
Oh? What's that?

BLACKBIRD

Your eyesight's bad.

CHANTECLER, *softly, to the Blackbird*
You joke about our fears.

BLACKBIRD

To see more clearly. . .

BRIFFAUT
Well?

BLACKBIRD

Pin back your ears.

BRIFFAUT
disappearing with an angry growl

Humph!

CHANTECLER
after a pause, to the Blackbird, who goes back up
to his cage and looks over the wall
Is he gone?

BLACKBIRD
Far gone.

CHANTECLER, *going to Patou's corner*
Come out, Madame

PHEASANT, *appearing in the doorway*
Escaped, rebellious, yes... the dog was right.
But my race is great, and I'm proud as well as free—
A woodland pheasant!
She comes out with a leap.

BLACKBIRD
And clearly not a peasant.

PHEASANT, *walking about feverishly*
My home is deep in the woods, where the poacher goes—

CHANTECLER
That fool who'd put a jewel in a setting of lead!

PHEASANT
I live where the sunlight pierces through thick leaves.
But I come from somewhere else. From where? From Persia?
China? No one knows. But rest assured
That I was born to shimmer against the blue,
Among green branches swollen with sandarac,
And not to be chased through thorns by a maniac!
Was I the Phoenix? the sacred Chinese hen?
Who was it brought me here? and how and when?
The Legend is unclear; I'm free to choose
My birthplace. So I've chosen Colchis, where
I must have sailed, on Jason's fist, for Greece.
I'm golden. Why can't I have been the Fleece?

PATOU
Who, you?

PHEASANT
I, the Pheasant!

PATOU, *gently correcting her*
Hen.

PHEASANT
My race!
I represent it, since I took its purple
Shield. Yes, the fate that I endured
So long—a dead leaf set beside a ruby—
Seemed one day decidely too pale,
And so I stole the dazzling plumes of the male.

And I was right, for I wear them better than he.
On me the golden breastplate curves and glows,
The epaulettes of green have a dainty air,
And a simple uniform has grace and flair.

> CHANTECLER
She's absolutely stunning.

> PATOU, *to himself*
>> Spare me the sight!
He's not going to fall in love with a transvestite?

> BLACKBIRD, *hopping down from his cage*
I've got to tell the Guinea-Hen that there's
A golden bird in town. She'll have a fit.
She'll want to invite her.
> *to Chantecler*
> Well, I'm off for a walk.
>> *He leaves.*

> CHANTECLER, *approaching the Pheasant*
And so you come from the east, just like the Day?

> PHEASANT
My life has the gay abandon of poetry.
If I'm from the East, it must be Hungary.

> PATOU, *to himself, heart-brokenly*
A gypsy!

> PHEASANT
> *to Chantecler, making the colors play on her throat*
> Have you noticed these two colors?
Dawn and I are the only ones who wear them.
Princess of brush and Queen of the glades, I bear
The golden mark of those who seek adventure.
Feeling homesick, I took the withered iris
Stalks at the edge of a pool as a rustling palace.
How I love the woods! And when Fall brings
The scent of drying leaves and dying twigs...

> PATOU, *in consternation*
She's mad.

> PHEASANT
> I'm wild, as if I were a branch
A sirocco were twisting, lashing...

CHANTECLER
who has begun to circle her, wing drooping—as the
Blackbird did in imitating him—and to make a soft
sound low in his throat

Co-o-o-ck...

The Pheasant watches him. He takes this for encouragement
and continues more strongly, still circling her.

Co-o-o-ck...

PHEASANT
I'd better tell you right away:
If all of this is done for me...

CHANTECLER, *stopping*

All what?

PHEASANT
The eyes, the drooping wing, the "Co-o-o-ck"...

CHANTECLER

But I...

PHEASANT
It's quite well done, except it doesn't do
A thing for me.

CHANTECLER, *somewhat baffled*
Madame...

PHEASANT
I understand,
Of course. When one is *The* Most Famous Rooster,
One assumes that every hen in the world
Will preen her feathers hoping just to catch
One's eye between two crows. One's ego never
Falters, even if the lady comes
As a guest and isn't quite your apron type,
Who thinks there's nothing more to life than eggs.

CHANTECLER
But—

PHEASANT
I don't fall in love without a squawk!
Besides, for me, you're too much... Cock of the Walk.

CHANTECLER
Of the walk?

PHEASANT
Too spoiled. Give me a simpler creature,
One for whom I'd be the whole of the world.

CHANTECLER
But look—

PHEASANT
To love a famous Rooster—no,
I'm not so feminine as that.

CHANTECLER, *after a pause*
                                        At least
We can go for a walk, Madame.

PHEASANT
                                Of course. As friends.

CHANTECLER
Old friends.

PHEASANT, *quickly*
        Not old... just plain.

CHANTECLER, *still more quickly*
                        No, no... never plain.
        going to her
A look at the farmyard? Take my wing.

PHEASANT
                                Let's go.

CHANTECLER, *stopping before the trough*
Now, this is awful. The latest kind of trough,
In galvanized tin. But all the rest is splendid,
Beautified by use. The henhouse roof,
The stable door...

BLACKBIRD, *entering; to himself*
                The Guinea-Hen is wild!

PHEASANT
to Chantecler, looking around her
You live in peace here, fearing nothing?

CHANTECLER
                                        Yes.
The owner is a vegetarian,
An amazing man, who loves all animals.

He gives them names from the poets. There, the donkey's
Midas. Io, that's the calf.

                    BLACKBIRD, *watching them*
                                          Look out,
He's dropping names.

                    PHEASANT, *pointing to the Blackbird*
                         And he?

                         CHANTECLER
                              The wit of the place.

                         PHEASANT

What does he do?

                         CHANTECLER
                         Keeps busy.

                         PHEASANT
                              Doing what?

                         CHANTECLER
Making sure he never looks like a fool.
That's quite a job.

                         PHEASANT
                         But not a nice one.

                    They move away.

                         BLACKBIRD
          glancing at the Pheasant's scarlet breastplate
                                          Keep
Away! It's scarlet fever—look at her chest!

                    CHANTECLER, *continuing the tour*
The haystack. Then the old wall. Whenever I sing,
It oozes lizards, and the haystack leans still more.
I sing from over there, where I scratch the earth,
And when I'm done, I drink from this old bowl.

                    PHEASANT, *smiling*
Your song is so important, then?

                    CHANTECLER, *gravely*
                                          Oh, yes.

                         PHEASANT

But why?

CHANTECLER
I keep the reason secret.

PHEASANT

Let's

Suppose I asked to know it.

CHANTECLER
changing the subject, pointing to a stack of branches in a corner
Those are friends,

The firewood sticks.

PHEASANT
They're stolen from my woods!
—So what they say is true: you have a secret?

CHANTECLER, *sharply*

Yes, Madame.

PHEASANT
It seems the subject's closed.

CHANTECLER
climbing on the wall at the back
From here you can see the rest of my domain,
Out to the kitchen garden where, at night,
They bring a snake whose head is a waterfall.

PHEASANT

You mean that's all?

CHANTECLER
That's all.

PHEASANT

So you believe

Some eggplants mark the edge of the world?

CHANTECLER

No.

PHEASANT
A flying wedge of emigrants goes by
And you don't dream of far horizons?

CHANTECLER

No.

PHEASANT
But all these things you've shown are poor and sad.

CHANTECLER
To me the constant wonder is their richness.

PHEASANT
What? They always stay the same.

CHANTECLER
                                                                They don't!

There's always something new beneath the sun
Because of the sun. She changes things.

PHEASANT
                                                                Who's "she"?

CHANTECLER
The Light! That geranium plant on the window-sill
Is never the same red twice. That fine old shoe
That spits out straw... the wooden comb that hangs
Among the overalls and keeps the hair
Of the lawn between her teeth... the fork they place
In the corner, as if in disgrace, who sleeps while standing
Up and dreams of hay... the old wood bowl
Whose rim becomes a world the ant can go
Around in eighty seconds—none of these
Remain the same! And I, Madame, I've had
A whole lifetime in which a hanging rake
Or a vase of flowers gives me the kind of joy
That never dies, and a morning-glory holds
The power to hypnotize.

PHEASANT, *thoughtfully*
                                                You have a soul,
I feel. But how can a soul be formed so far
From life and drama, shaped behind a wall
Where a tomcat sleeps?

CHANTECLER
                                If one can see and suffer,
One knows all. An insect's death contains
All tragedy, a patch of sky all stars.

OLD HEN, *appearing*
The sky's known best of all by the water in the well.

CHANTECLER
introducing her before the lid falls back

My nurse.

PHEASANT

Oh, yes?

OLD HEN, *winking*
A handsome rooster, eh?

PHEASANT, *going to her*
And one whose mind has room for... many things

CHANTECLER, *going to Patou*
My friend, there's a hen with whom one can really talk.

*Offstage are heard piercing cries
and a tumultuous chattering.*

VOICES, *coming nearer*

Ah!

BLACKBIRD
We're going to have the Guinea Hen.

GUINEA HEN, *running to the Pheasant*
Oh, Lord! She's divine! — We simply *flew* to meet you!

*All circle around the Pheasant.
Chatter. Cries. Clucking.*

CHANTECLER, *to himself*
What a walk she has!

He looks at his Hens.
Not like my Hens.

Irritated, he calls to them.
Hens! You walk as if you all had corns!
As if you were walking on eggs— your own, at that!

PATOU

He's falling hard.

GUINEA HEN
presenting her son to the Pheasant
My son, the Guinea Cock.

GUINEA COCK, *admiring the Pheasant*
How blond she is!

A HEN, *softly*
Like butter.

CHANTECLER, *sharply, to the Hens*
                                    Go inside.

PHEASANT, *pleasantly but regretfully*

Already?

CHANTECLER
Yes. They go to bed quite early.

The Hens start to climb the stair to the henhouse.

A HEN, *a bit put out*

Yes, we're going in.

PHEASANT, *amazed*
                            My word, by a stair?

GUINEA HEN, *to the Pheasant*
My dear, I feel we're going to be great friends.

CHANTECLER
to himself, watching the Pheasant
She stand out, wearing those regal clothes. She makes
The others look as if they were dressed in smocks.

PHEASANT, *excusing herself to the Guinea Hen*
Tonight I must go back to my forest shelter.

GUINEA HEN, *devastated*

No!

A shot is heard in the distance.

PATOU
They're still out hunting.

GUINEA HEN
                                    Better stay.

CHANTECLER, *quickly*
That's right. We'll keep you captive till tomorrow.

PHEASANT

Where would I sleep?

PATOU, *indicating his kennel*
                            My bachelor's quarters, there.

PHEASANT

I, to sleep beneath a roof!

PATOU, *insisting*

Go on.

PHEASANT

And you?

PATOU

A dog's life means you often sleep
Outdoors.

PHEASANT, *resignedly*

I'll stay until tomorrow, then.

GUINEA HEN, *shrieking*

Tomorrow! Darling! Lord, tomorrow!

ALL, *frightened*

What?

GUINEA COCK

Tomorrow, that's the day of her soiree.

GUINEA HEN, *impetuously, to the Pheasant*

It's quite impromptu, dear. Why not drop in
And have a snail? The Peacock—

CHANTECLER

who has climbed the stairs to look over the whole yard

Not so loud.

The night is breathing shadows.

commandingly

Each of you

Is in his place?

GUINEA HEN, *more softly, to the Pheasant*

We'll have the Peacock there.
Below the berry bushes, that's the spot.

CHANTECLER

The Turkeys on their perch?

GUINEA HEN, *same business*

We start at six.

CHANTECLER

The Ducks beneath their pointed roof?

GUINEA HEN, *same*

I think
We'll even have the Turtle.

PHEASANT

Oh, you will?

CHANTECLER, *who has reached the top step*
Everyone is sheltered?

GUINEA COCK, *ironic*

So, you give
Commands at every step?

CHANTECLER

Yes, sir. — All Chicks
Beneath a wing? — The humblest home must keep up
Discipline.

GUINEA HEN
still insisting that the Pheasant come the next day

The Tufted Hen has said
She'll bring the Cock.
to Chantecler

We'd be just thrilled!

CHANTECLER

But I—

TUFTED HEN
authoritatively, poking her head out of the henhouse
Of course you'll go.

CHANTECLER
No.

PHEASANT
at the foot of the stairs, watching him

Yes.

CHANTECLER

But why?

PHEASANT
Because you told the other one No.

CHANTECLER

Ah...?

PATOU

Well, I'll be a son of a lady! Look at that.

CHANTECLER, *hesitating*

I could...

PATOU

He's bending. Now she'll call the tune.

OLD HEN, *appearing*
To make reed pipes, you start by bending reeds.

The lid falls, and Night begins gently to do the same.

CHANTECLER

Well, I...

A VOICE

Let's sleep.

TURKEY, *solemnly, on his perch*
Quandoque dormitat.

BLACKBIRD

No, dormi*tory*.

CHANTECLER, *firmly, to the Pheasant*
No, I won't. Good night.

PHEASANT, *a bit vexed*

Good night.

She enters the kennel with a brusque leap.
Night grows a deeper blue.

PATOU
settling to sleep in front of the kennel
Let's sleep till the sky is rosy, like...
Just like... a puppy's tummy...

GUINEA HEN, *sleeping*
We start at six...

BLACKBIRD, *sleeping too*

Tew-tew.

CHANTECLER, *still at the top of the stairs*
They're all asleep.
He spies a chick sneaking out.
A chick out of bed?

He dashes down after him and shoos him back.

Hey, you!

Finding himself before the kennel, he calls softly
Pheasant...

PHEASANT
deep in the straw, in a sleepy voice
What?

CHANTECLER, *after a pause*
It's nothing.
pauses again, then sighs
Nothing.

Regretfully he climbs back up the stairs.

PHEASANT

How can I sleep...

PATOU, *quite asleep now*
As rosy as... as rrrrosy...

PHEASANT
...Underneath a roof? My tastes are more
Sophis...

CHANTECLER, *disappearing into the henhouse*
I'm home.
in a fading voice
It's time to close...to close...

PHEASANT, *one final effort*
Sophis... sophis-ticated...

*Her head, which had lifted for a moment,
falls back and disappears in the straw.*

CHANTECLER'S VOICE, *nearly asleep*
...Close my eyes.

Silence. On the wall two green eyes light up.

CAT

And open mine!

*Immediately two more eyes, yellow, light up
in the darkness, on the roof of the barn.*

A VOICE
And mine.

Two more yellow eyes light up.

ANOTHER VOICE
And mine.

Two more yellow eyes light up.

ANOTHER VOICE
And mine.

The silhouettes of three Screech Owls can now be seen.

A SCREECH OWL
Two eyes of green?

CAT
erect on the wall, watching the other phosphorescent eyes
Six eyes of gold?

SCREECH OWL
On the wall?

CAT
On the barn?
He calls.
Oh, Owls!

SCREECH OWL
Who howls?

CAT
It's the cat who's calling...

ALL THREE SCREECH OWLS
Caterwauling...

BLACKBIRD, *awakening*
What's this noise? It's appalling!

1st SCREECH OWL
Conspiracy—to plot his fate.

CAT
Tonight?

SCREECH OWLS
That's right.

CAT

That's great.

SCREECH OWLS
How true! How true! How true!

CAT

What place?

SCREECH OWLS
The holly grove will do! will do!

CAT

What time?

SCREECH OWLS
At eight. He's through! He's through! He's through!

BATS cut zigzags through the air.

1st SCREECH OWL

Bats with whom the darkness juggles!

CAT
                                                                    They

Are with us, too?

SCREECH OWLS
They too.

1st SCREECH OWL
                                    And Mole whose claws

I hear!

CAT

Is she with us?

SCREECH OWLS
                                        She too.

CAT
calling toward the door of the house
                                                            Cuckoo

Who lives in the clock, call out the hour of eight!

1st SCREECH OWL

Is he with us?

CAT
He too. You'll also find
Some birds of the day who stand on the Nightbirds' side.

TURKEY
*coming forward from a furtive group of barnyard birds
who have only pretended to go to sleep*
It's set for tonight, dear round-eyes? You'll be there?

SCREECH OWLS
We will. And all the other round-eyes, too.

BLACKBIRD, *to himself*
I'd love to see that.

PATOU, *while sleeping*
R-r-r-r...

CAT, *reassuring the Nightbirds*
The Dog...he growls
When he dreams.

CHANTECLER, *inside the henhouse*
Co-o-o-ck...

SCREECH OWLS, *terrified*
It's he! It's he! It's he!

TURKEY
You'd better flee.

1st SCREECH OWL
No need for that. The night
Is black. We'll shut our eyes and disappear.

They close their eyes. Night thickens.

CHANTECLER
appearing at the top of the stairs
Did you hear something, Blackbird?

BLACKBIRD
Yes, old boy.

OWLS, *frightened*
What's that?

BLACKBIRD, *melodramatically*
A dark conspiracy...and you're
The object. Tremble!

CHANTECLER, *reassured*
Clown!
He re-enters.

OWLS, *reopening their eyes*
He's back inside.

BLACKBIRD, *satisfied*
And no one was betrayed.

A SCREECH OWL
The Blackbird, then,
Is with us too?

BLACKBIRD
Oh, no. But I'd love to watch.

A SCREECH OWL
A Nightbird never eats a blackbird. Come.

BLACKBIRD
The password?

A SCREECH OWL
Ebony and Infamy!

PHEASANT, *sticking her head from the kennel*
I'm choking here beneath this roof...
seeing the Nightbirds
Oh!

She pulls back quickly but stays on the lookout.

SCREECH OWLS
Ssssh!
*They quickly close their eyes, then,
hearing nothing more, reopen them.*
It's nothing. Let's be gone.

A VOICE
from the group of barnyard birds who have remained awake
Good luck!

1st SCREECH OWL
We thank you. Tell us, though, why all of you
Are on our side.

CAT
Ah, night brings out those things
That one has hidden from oneself. The reason I
Don't like the Cock? Because the Dog... does.

TURKEY
And I, the Turkey, *propter hoc:* I can't
Abide that the chick I taught is now a cock.

DUCK
I, the Duck, don't like him because his feet
Have no web. When he walks, he leaves the stars in his ebb.

A PULLET
I don't like the Cock because his traits
Are painted in red and gold on so many plates.

ANOTHER PULLET
And his statue stands on every weathervane.

ANOTHER PULLET
I don't like the Cock because I'm plain.

A SCREECH OWL, *to a large Pullet*
And Capon, you?

CAPON, *dryly*
I just don't like the Cock.

CUCKOO
starting to sound the hour of eight from his little house
Cuckoo!

1st SCREECH OWL
It's time.

CUCKOO
Cuckoo!

2nd SCREECH OWL
Let's go.

CUCKOO
Cuckoo!

A white ray begins to bathe one side of the yard.

1st SCREECH OWL
The moon!

CUCKOO
Cuckoo!

1st SCREECH OWL, *opening his wings*
Let's cleave our way through the blue...

CUCKOO
Cuckoo!

THE MOLE
whose head suddenly appears from the ground
...And cut through the dark brown earth.

1st SCREECH OWL
Oh, look,

The Mole.

CUCKOO
Cuckoo!

1st SCREECH OWL
And why do you hate him, Mole?

MOLE
I hate him because I've never seen him.

CUCKOO
Cuckoo!

1st SCREECH OWL
And you, Cuckoo? Can you say?

CUCKOO, *sounding the last stroke*
Because he never
Needs someone to wind him up. — Cuckoo!

1st SCREECH OWL
And we don't like...

2nd SCREECH OWL
It's time to go!

1st SCREECH OWL, *as all the Owls open their wings*
...the Cock

Because...

2nd SCREECH OWL
They'll all be waiting! Heavens above!

They all fly off. Silence.

PHEASANT, *slowly emerging from the kennel*
And what I'm starting to feel for him... is love.

The curtain falls.

ACT TWO

The
Morning
of the
Cock

THE SCENE: The promontory of a little hill.

Clumps of hollies. A garden left to grow wild. A place that is melancholy at night, when weeds rustle on the trodden path. But what can be seen from here, when day has risen...

Is the Valley. The little valley with a capital V, the essence of the countryside, with its rivers, its nobility, its perfection.

A calm horizon, limiting desires but not dreams. Slim poplars. A beautiful little hill that lies stretched out like a beast with a village at its withers.

The sky is the sky of home. And when some humble chimney begins to smoke in a corner, one will think one is seeing the pipe of Corot.

AT RISE: THE NIGHTBIRDS, of all sizes and species, form a large circle and rise in tiers upon the stones, brambles, and branches; THE CAT crouches in the grass; THE BLACKBIRD hops on a bundle of sticks.

When the curtain rises, deep night. All the Nightbirds are immobile, black silhouettes with closed eyes. The Grand Duke, perched on a tree trunk, is the commanding figure. Only the Screech Owl has his phosphorescent eyes wide open. He calls the roll, and with each name, two large round luminous eyes open in the blackness.

SCREECH OWL, calling

Strix!
> *Two eyes open.*
> > Scops!
> > > *Two eyes open.*
> > > > Grand Duke!
> > > > > *Two eyes open.*
> > > > > > Middle Duke!
> > > > > > > *Two eyes open.*
> > > > > > > > Little Duke!
> > > > > > > > *Two eyes open.*

ONE NIGHTBIRD, to another

The Grand Duke is presiding.

SCREECH OWL, continuing
Owl of the Yew!

The Wall! the Apse! the Cloister!

At each name, two eyes open.

A NIGHTBIRD, *to another who enters*
It's roll-call.

THE OTHER
I know. We open our eyes.

SCREECH OWL
Surnia! Alba!
Nyctea!
Three more pairs of eyes open.
Brachyote!
When no eyes open, he repeats
Brachyote!

A NIGHTBIRD
He's on his way. He stopped to eat a linnet.

BRACHYOTE, *arriving*
Here!

SCREECH OWL
When it's about the Cock, they all
Are here.

ALL THE NIGHTBIRDS, *with one voice*
All!

SCREECH OWL
Asio!
Two eyes open.
Caparacoch!
No eyes having opened, he repeats insistently
Ca - pa - ra - coch! — Well!

CAPARACOCH
arriving out of breath, opening his eyes and making an excuse
I live quite far away.

SCREECH OWL, *dryly*
Then one should hurry.
looking around him
I think they're all here now.
calls
Bubo! Bubette!
Now all the eyes are open.

GRAND DUKE, *solemnly*

Before we start, let's say—but softly, please—
The cry that makes us One.

ALL

Long live the Night!

Their chorus is urgent, savage, and mysterious,
interspersed with the beating of wings and
long cries in the night; all speak in rapid
succession, with a fierce rocking movement:

GRAND DUKE

Long live the pliant, blessed Night
When all are sleeping, and our flight
   Is soft as breath;
On padded wing we wheel and veer,
And thus the partridge does not hear
   Her coming death.

SCREECH OWL

Long live the Night accommodating,
Who, when one is immolating
   Baby rabbits,
Lets one spread the grass with gore
Without acquiring skills of war
   Or a hero's habits.

OLD HORNED OWL

Long live the shadows, dense and black.

WOOD OWL

The hush that lets each juicy crack
   Of bone be heard.

A BARN OWL

The air so cool our glasses steam
When squirted with a warm, red stream
   Of blood from a bird.

ANOTHER

Long live the crag where terrors ooze.

ANOTHER SCREECH OWL

The cross-road where, whenever one hooos
   And hoots...

ANOTHER WOOD OWL
. . .and wails.

Miaows and screeches. . .

A BARN OWL
. . .shrills and skrees,

GRAND DUKE

Even skeptics fall to their knees.

ALL
The Night prevails!

GRAND DUKE

Long live the Weaver of dark disguise,
The peerless Night, whose stars comprise
Her one mistake.

SCREECH OWL

But they can only watch in vain
When our retractile claws contain
A neck to break.

GRAND DUKE

Long live the Night, when one repays
The goldfinch for his graceful ways.
For when the shroud
Of darkness once again is drawn,
Then Night holds Beauty as a pawn,
Who screams aloud.

WOOD OWL

We want a choice of whom we kill.

GRAND DUKE

And darkness gives our eyes the skill
To scan the trees
Until the bluest jay in the nest,
The dove who has the whitest breast,
Are ours to seize.

A BARN OWL

Long live the hour when broken eggs
Are cups in which we drain the dregs
Of a future race.

SCREECH OWL
The hour to whisper and prepare,
So all our crimes will seem to bear
        An innocent face.

GRAND DUKE
Long live the Night, where none dispute
Our reign of fear!
                    SCREECH OWL
                    For when we hoot...
                    AN OWL
            And howl our spite...
                    ALL BARN OWLS
And ululate...
                    ALL OWLS
                    ...and squall and squawk,
                    GRAND DUKE
There's goose-flesh even on the hawk!
                    ALL
        Long live the Night!

GRAND DUKE
And now, in his robe of russet silk, let us
Hear the Screech Owl.

SEVERAL VOICES
Ssssh!

BLACKBIRD, *on his pile of sticks*
                    Charming party.

SCREECH OWL, *oratorically*
Birds of the Night!

GRAND DUKE, *to his neighbor*
                    We have the blackest corner
And the moldiest tree. On the right, old flower pots.
On the left, between the hollies, quite a view.
Whoever picked the spot, I don't know who...

ALL NIGHTBIRDS
Whooo! Whooo!

GRAND DUKE
...Has chosen very well.

SCREECH OWL

Birds of the Night!

AN OWL
Look! the mole is here?

SEVERAL VOICES

Ssssh!

ANOTHER OWL
She came below the grass...

BLACKBIRD, *hopping*

By subway.

GRAND DUKE, *to his neighbor*
That's the Blackbird?

BLACKBIRD, *coming forward*
Yes, Duke. Those two agates,

That's the Cat.

GRAND DUKE
I hear him lick his paws.

SCREECH OWL, *resuming*
Birds of the Night! Because tonight we all
Take pride in being possessors of the evil eye...

ALL NIGHTBIRDS
sniggering and rocking in their characteristic manner

Ha! Ha!

GRAND DUKE
opening his wings to impose silence

Sssh!

BLACKBIRD
My eye is shrewd, that's all.
I help, but I don't take sides. Just like an artist.

AN OWL
To take no side, that means you side with us.

BLACKBIRD
Oh, really, now! So black and white, these owls.

SCREECH OWL, *completing his sentence*
Let's state our case with a frankly malevolent beak:
The Cock is a thief!

ALL
A thief! He steals from us!

BLACKBIRD
But what?

GRAND DUKE
Our health! and joy!

BLACKBIRD
Oh, that's too much.

But how?

SCREECH OWL
He sings!

GRAND DUKE
His singing gives us swollen
Spleen and brings on cardiac arrest.
Because the Cock announces!

BLACKBIRD, *hopping*
Yes, the light.

All make a threatening move. The Blackbird,
frightened, hides behind his pile of sticks.

GRAND DUKE, *sharply*
Don't say that word! Whenever it's spoken, Night
Can feel an itching underneath her wing.

BLACKBIRD, *prudently correcting himself*
The brightness.

All move again. Same business from the Blackbird.

SCREECH OWL
Not that word! It grates just like
The striking of a match.

SCREECH OWL
Say instead: "The Cock
Announces. . . a folding back of the ebon cloth."

BLACKBIRD
But the day—

ALL
moving and crying with unspeakable pain
No, not that word!

GRAND DUKE
Say: "What will come."

BLACKBIRD
So what if he announces—

ALL
No!

BLACKBIRD
...The folding?

What is going to come... will come.

GRAND DUKE, *despairingly*
It's torture,

Clearly—

BLACKBIRD
Darkly!

GRAND DUKE
...torture, always being
Reminded that it's true.

ALL THE OWLS, *grimacing in pain*
True! True!

GRAND DUKE
He sings when night is still so fresh and sweet.

CRIES ON ALL SIDES
A thief! A thief!

GRAND DUKE
He cheats us...

ALL THE OWLS
Cheats us! Cheats us!

GRAND DUKE
...Out of the lovely piece of night that's left.

LITTLE DUKE
He makes us leave our watch beside the rabbit
Hutches!

SCREECH OWL
Leave our feasts of flesh!

WOOD OWL
                                                           Leave
Our sabbath rides upon a witch's fist!

GRAND DUKE
His song upsets our normal state.

SCREECH OWL
                                                           We start
To hurry with our evil.

GRAND DUKE
                            So we bungle.

AN OWL
When he sings, we know we're transitory.

BARN OWL
Knowing Night will start to lose her glory.

SCREECH OWL
Once his metal song has cut the night,
You squirm just like a worm inside an apple.

BLACKBIRD
who understands none of this, on his pile of sticks
Still, the other Cocks—

GRAND DUKE
                            Have harmless songs.
It's his that must be stifled.

ALL NIGHTBIRDS
flapping their wings, in a long plaint
                            Stifled! Stifled!

AN OWL
How to do it?

SCREECH OWL
The Blackbird helps our cause...

BLACKBIRD
Who, me?

SCREECH OWL
Yes, by mocking him.

ALL, *sniggering and rocking*

Ha! ha!

GRAND DUKE, *spreading his wings*

Sssh!

They resume their sinister immobility.

GRAND DUKE
But even so, his song is just
As hard on our digestion. Once he heard
The ridicule, it simply made him stronger.

ALL

How to do it?

SCREECH OWL
The Peacock, that old fool...

ALL, *sniggering and rocking*

Ha! ha!

GRAND DUKE, *opening his wings*

Sssh!

Immobility.

SCREECH OWL
...Is working too, by calling
Him passé. But that's no help: He sings
With even more conviction when he's out
Of style.

ALL

How to do it?

A BARN OWL

Cut his throat!

CRIES

Yes, death to the Cock!

AN OWL

Death to that
Aristocrat who plays the friend of the masses.

ANOTHER OWL
Wears a crest but says he's all for labor.

GRAND DUKE

Birds of the Night, arise!

All stand erect, wings open and eyes huge:
the night seems to heighten.

BLACKBIRD, *unaffected, playing the clown*
The midnight shift.

SCREECH OWL

Cut his throat? Once he appears, we're blind.

ALL, *moaning like an ancient chorus*

Alas!

AN OWL, *slyly*
How to cut his throat... from a distance?

GRAND DUKE

How?

A VOICE, *on a branch*
Duke! May I propose a plan?

GRAND DUKE

Scops! You may.

ALL
watching a little owl drop from the tree and come forward with small hops
Scops! our little Scops!

SCOPS, *bowing before the Grand Duke*
You know, o seer of Night, that in that pleasant
Garden there on the slope, a man they call
An... aviculturist, who raises birds
For meetings they call... agricultural,
Is breeding fancy cocks of every kind.
Now then, that patron of birds who are rare, the Peacock
—Who, with a voice that pierces ear-drums, cannot
Bear a voice that pierces darkness—this
Peacock, whose system is to lionize
The strange and new...

GRAND DUKE, *to his neighbor*
Especially if it's foreign.

SCOPS
...Dreams that tomorrow he will launch those cocks
In the kitchen garden...

ALL, *together, laughing*
At the Guinea Hen's affair!

SCOPS
...And let their splendor outshine Chantecler's
And deal it a fatal blow.

BLACKBIRD, *hopping*
A total eclipse!

SCREECH OWL
Those Cocks are always kept locked up.

SCOPS
Well,

Tonight, when a girl was opening the cage
And throwing corn to them in yellow showers.
I rose out of a tree, and when the girl...

AN OWL, *to his neighbor*
He's shrewd, that little Scops.

SCOPS
...Observed this bird

Of evil omen...

ALL, *sniggering and rocking*
Ha! ha!

GRAND DUKE, *opening his wings*
Sssh!

Immobility.

SCOPS
...She covered

Her face and ran away. And since the cage
Stayed open, tomorrow that whole gang will meet
With Chantecler...

ALL, *in a climactic snigger*
At the Guinea Hen's affair!

BLACKBIRD

He'll never go.

SCOPS
Oh, damn!

CAT, *phlegmatically*
Proceed. He'll go.

BLACKBIRD
looking at him, keeping his distance
And what do you know about it, little tiger?

CAT
I saw him falling for a Pheasant. I saw that he
Would go.

BLACKBIRD
When you're asleep, you don't miss a trick.

GRAND DUKE, *to Scops*
Let's say he goes, then.

SCOPS
Chantecler is famous,
But he's kept his country frankness. Once
He sees that...

BLACKBIRD, *prompting him*
Cocktail party.

SCOPS
And that whole crowd of...

BLACKBIRD
Phonies.

SCOPS
Fawning on those...

BLACKBIRD
Feather-brains.

SCOPS
...He's sure to say some things they'll have to challenge.

GRAND DUKE, *thrilled*
You think a cock-fight...?

SCOPS
Duke, that is my dream.

CAT
Suppose he wins?

SCOPS

Angora, one of those fancy
Cocks will be a real fighting cock,
Who's lean and tawny...

BLACKBIRD

seeing all the feathers ruffle up with joy
Well, that shook them up.

SCOPS

...One who's gouged the eyes of famous champions:
The White Pile Cock. And since, to cut his rivals'
Throats, this victor of battles all over the country
Wears two razors, one on each heel, attached
By human ingenuity, tomorrow
Chantecler will be quite dead, with both
His eyes pecked out.

SCREECH OWL, *enthusiastically*
We'll go to see his corpse!

GRAND DUKE

risen to his full height, formidable
We'll take his crest, that looked just like a piece
Of the dawn, and then, to celebrate, we'll eat it!

ALL

with a howl that ends in their fierce rocking and sniggering
We'll - eat - it! Ha-ha!

GRAND DUKE, *opening his wings*

Sssh!

Immobility.

SCOPS

And then...

BLACKBIRD, *hopping*
Stop! It's cock-a-mamie enough.

SCOPS

What is?

BLACKBIRD

What you propose. Good Lord! If I
Were one to take things seriously, I'd go
And tell the Cock. But I'll do no such thing,

He concludes with five little hops.
Because - I know - that things - will work out - nicely!

SCOPS, *ironically*

Very nicely.
He continues, more and more excited.
Then, tomorrow night,
If all those foreign cocks are not locked up,
We'll eat them, too, because they're of no more use!

GRAND DUKE, *in his neighbor's ear*
And then we'll eat the Blackbird for dessert.

BLACKBIRD, *who did not hear*

What's that?

SCOPS, *quickly*

Oh, nothing.
He continues, in a growing frenzy.
Then we'll—

DISTANT VOICE
Cock-a-doodle-doo!

Abrupt silence. Scops collapses as if mown down.
All the puffed Owls suddenly seem to be thinner.

ALL, *looking at each other and blinking*
What's that? What is it?
Suddenly they open their wings, calling to
one another in preparation for flight.
Grand Duke! Middle Duke!

Little Duke!

BLACKBIRD, *hopping from one to another*
You're leaving? What's the rush?

VOICE OF A NIGHTBIRD, *calling another one*
Asio!

BLACKBIRD
You still have lots of time before it's dawn.

A BARN OWL

Come on, Surnia!

ANOTHER, *calling*
Nyctea!

ANOTHER, *fluttering to join him*
Yes, my dear.

All of them stagger, tripping on their wings.

BLACKBIRD, *astounded*
They're stumbling.

NIGHTBIRDS
blinking their eyes, with little starts of pain
Oh, it hurts! . . . Ay! . . . Ay!

BLACKBIRD
Sounds like eye trouble.

GRAND DUKE
Staying to the last, he stumbles over himself
and cries with pain and rage:
How did that pernicious
Cock acquire a voice that's so malicious?

He flies off heavily.

VOICES OF THE NIGHTBIRDS
calling in the distance
Strix!

BLACKBIRD
watching as they fly through the branches
and then into the blue gulf of the valley
They're calling!

DISTANT VOICE
Scops!

BLACKBIRD
leaning to look over the valley,
where the black wings pass and grow smaller
They turn. . . waver. . .
Dip. . .

A VOICE, *calling and dying in the distance*
Owl of the Wall! of the Yew! of the. . .

BLACKBIRD
Gone!
He looks around, hops, and then clowns immediately.
It's supper time. Bring us a nice cold cricket!

>   *At this moment the Pheasant leaps from the brush*
>   *and drops in front of him.*

You!

>   PHEASANT, *panting, tragic*
>   I ran... and you were there... I'm terrified!

Well! You must have heard their secret.
You, his friend?

>   BLACKBIRD
>   *cheerfully rummaging in the moss*
>   Bring us a haunch of locust!

>   PHEASANT

I was watching... from a distance... I was in a ditch...
>   *in an anguished voice*

Well?

>   BLACKBIRD, *with genuine surprise*
>   Well what?

>   PHEASANT
>   This plot!

>   BLACKBIRD, *calm*
>   It came off nicely.

>   PHEASANT, *astounded*

What?

>   BLACKBIRD
>   The shadows were designer blue,

And all the owls were speaking purple prose.

>   PHEASANT, *with a bound*

Good Lord! They planned his death!

>   BLACKBIRD
>   No, his demise.

That's not as bad.

>   PHEASANT
>   But...

>   BLACKBIRD
>   Don't carry on!

It's true the Screech Owl sounds like a feudal lord,
But I believe his plans are simply... futile.

PHEASANT

Those owls...?

BLACKBIRD
They played it well, but it's all played out.

PHEASANT

What is?

BLACKBIRD
Melodrama.

PHEASANT
Oh?

BLACKBIRD, *pityingly*

They wear

Their eyebrows all the way around their eyes.
Really, it's too much. And then their plot:
They didn't make it up, they dug it up.

PHEASANT, *pacing feverishly*
I never can be sure if someone's joking.

BLACKBIRD, *winking*
Yes, the Gypsy... how well you play the part...

PHEASANT
If he were really in trouble, you wouldn't laugh.
Those bandits...

BLACKBIRD
Babblers! Rattling little tin swords!
The Pirates of Palaver.

PHEASANT

Yes, but the Screech Owl?

BLACKBIRD

He was a howl.

PHEASANT
The Grand Duke, then?

BLACKBIRD

A pair

Of headlights switched on and off by a trick: Click-click.
And as for that Bubette, the naughty girl,
She runs hers on acetylene.

PHEASANT, *bewildered by the raillery*

You mean...?

BLACKBIRD

I mean the owls' big plot isn't worth a hoot.

PHEASANT

Really? I was so scared.

BLACKBIRD

Seeing danger

Everywhere will only give you ulcers.
Why is the ostrich famous for his good
Digestion? It's because his head is always
Buried. All is well!

PHEASANT
letting herself take comfort from his optimism
Oh?

BLACKBIRD

Besides,

No one is doing tragedy any longer.

PHEASANT

Shouldn't Chantecler be warned?

BLACKBIRD

He'd go

And challenge them. It would come to blows.

PHEASANT, *quickly*

That's true.

BLACKBIRD

When an acorn falls, we mustn't holler "Timber!"

PHEASANT

Yes, you make good sense.

BLACKBIRD

Daughter of the Woods,

I do.

CHANTECLER'S VOICE, *outside*
Cock—...

PHEASANT, *starting*
It's he.

CHANTECLER
appearing at the left, between the hollies,
calling from the distance
Who's there?

PHEASANT
Me!

CHANTECLER, *still from a distance*

Alone?

PHEASANT, *giving the Blackbird a look*
Yes.

BLACKBIRD, *getting the point*
I'm going. Time for supper.

PHEASANT, *softly, to the Blackbird*

Well?

BLACKBIRD, *signalling her not to speak*
Ssssh!
He starts to exit right, as if summoning a waiter.
Wood! a woodlouse, please!

PHEASANT

I shouldn't tell him?

BLACKBIRD
before disappearing behind the flowerpots
Keep your pretty beak shut!

CHANTECLER, *coming to the Pheasant*
You're up already?

PHEASANT
To see the dawn.

CHANTECLER, *starting*
Ah?

PHEASANT
I'm very virtuous, my friend.

CHANTECLER, *sighing*
Yes.

PHEASANT, *a bit maliciously*
What's wrong with you?

CHANTECLER
I didn't sleep well.

PHEASANT

Oh?

A pause.

CHANTECLER
Will you be going to the Guinea Hen's affair?

PHEASANT
I'm staying over just because of that.

CHANTECLER
Ah, yes...
      A pause.
        I loathe her.

PHEASANT
Come to her party.

CHANTECLER

No.

PHEASANT
All right. Let's say goodbye.

CHANTECLER
        No.

PHEASANT

Then come

To the party and see me there.

CHANTECLER
        No.

PHEASANT

You won't?

CHANTECLER
Oh, yes. I'll go. But it makes me angry.

PHEASANT

Why?

CHANTECLER
Because it's giving in.

PHEASANT
Oh, that's not giving in.

CHANTECLER

No?

PHEASANT, *softly coming closer to him*
What would be, though...

CHANTECLER, *alarmed at her approach*
What?

PHEASANT

...Would be

To tell me just a bit about the secret.

CHANTECLER, *trembling*
The secret of my song?

PHEASANT
Yes.

CHANTECLER
Pheasant of Gold!

My secret?

PHEASANT, *coaxing*
Sometimes, when I'm at the edge of the wood,
I've heard you singing in the early light.

CHANTECLER, *flattered*

Oh?

My song has reached your little ears?

PHEASANT

Yes.

CHANTECLER, *turning away violently*
My secret! Never!

PHEASANT
You're not nice.

CHANTECLER

No.

I'm wretched.

PHEASANT, *reciting languidly*
The Cock and the Pheasant Hen: a fable.

>   CHANTECLER, *softly*
A Cock was in love with a Pheasant Hen...

>   PHEASANT
>   To whom

He would tell nothing.

>   CHANTECLER
>   Moral: ...

>   PHEASANT
>   He was hateful.

>   CHANTECLER, *close to her*
Moral: There are silken rustles in your gown.

>   PHEASANT
Moral: You are too familiar.
>   *She pulls away from him.*
>   Go
And find a hen in a housedress.

>   CHANTECLER, *stamping his foot*
>   Oh! I'm angry!

>   PHEASANT
Don't be angry. Come now, sing: Cock—...

>   *They are beak to beak.*

>   CHANTECLER, *furiously*
Cock!

>   PHEASANT
>   Oh, no. Sing better than that.

>   CHANTECLER, *in a long, tender coo*
>   Co-o-o-ck...

>   PHEASANT
Now look at me and do not laugh. Your secret...

>   CHANTECLER
What?

>   PHEASANT
>   You're burning to tell me.

>   CHANTECLER
>   Yes, I feel
That I am going to tell, and that it's wrong.

It's all because her head is dressed in gold.
>   *He goes to her abruptly.*
Will you be worthy, at least, of taking the part?
Does the red of your breast go all the way to your heart?

PHEASANT

Tell me!

CHANTECLER
>   Pheasant, look at me and try
To learn, from all the signs, the work of which
My body is the symbol. Start to find
My destiny in my design. Observe
That I am fashioned like a trumpet, curved in
Like a kind of living hunting-horn,
Made for sound to roll and echo in me
Just as clearly as the duck is made
For swimming. Now! Consider next that when
I scratch the earth, with eagerness and pride,
I always seem to look for something.

PHEASANT
>   Grain,

I would imagine?

CHANTECLER
>   No. I've never looked
For that. Sometimes I find it, but it's just
A serendipity I toss to my hens.

PHEASANT
Well then, what do you look for when you scratch?

CHANTECLER
The place to make a stand. Because I always
Plant myself before I sing. Observe!

PHEASANT
That's right, and then you ruffle up your feathers.

CHANTECLER
I never sing until my eight sharp claws
Have cleared away the weeds and kicked the stones
And reached deep down to find the sweet black soil.
Then, placed in touch with the earth I love, I sing.
And Pheasant, that is half the mystery
Already, half the secret of the song I sing,
Whose notes are not composed or learned but come

From the native soil directly, just like a sap.
And when that sap begins to rise in me,
When I can feel the genius, when I'm sure,
That's the hour when dawn is hesitating
Just below the rim. Trembling, then,
With a shiver that comes from the leaves and the grass and runs
To the very tips of my wings, I feel that I
Am chosen, so I arch my trumpet body,
Curve the curving horn a little more.
Earth speaks in me as in a sounding-shell;
No longer just a bird, I am the bell
Of some great speaking-trumpet, lifted high,
Through which the cry of earth can reach the sky.

PHEASANT

Chantecler!

CHANTECLER
This cry that mounts from earth
Is such a cry of love for light's rebirth;
A fierce and roaring cry, a mighty "Yea"
For all who miss that golden thing, the Day,
And need her touch: the pine-tree upon its bark,
The twisted forest path upon its dark
Veneer of moss; the wheat on every spear;
The pebble around its tiny hemisphere;
The cry of all who miss their flame or crest
Or image: grasses wet with dew request
A rainbow on each green tip, and woods implore
A fire to light each gloomy corridor;
This cry that climbs through me to reach toward space
Wells up from all who feel they're in disgrace,
Cast down in some abyss by the sun they love
As punishment for crimes they know not of;
The cry of cold and weariness and fright
Of all the helpless victims left to Night;
Of roses trembling, lonely down in the black;
Of hay not safe and dry within the stack;
Of tools the farmers left outside as prey
To creeping rust; of whiteness that has no way
To show the world its soul is dazzling white;
The cry of animals who feel no spite
And need no shroud to hide their deeds from view,
Of streams that bear no murky residue;
And even—Night, your very ranks defect!—
Of puddles wanting sunbeams they can reflect

And mud that yearns to dry and join the soil;
The cry of wheat and barley fields who toil
To push their spikes aloft in golden towers;
Of trees who cannot get their fill of flowers;
Of grapes in green who want a coat of plum;
Of bridges lying in wait for a step to come,
Their timbers hoping soon to be gently stirred
With shadow-patterns cast by leaf and bird;
Of all who want to shed their crepe and serve
Again, to be a river's glinting curve,
A sunny bench, a stone that warms a place
For hands to rest or ants to run their race;
It rises up, this fervent cry for light,
From all of Health and Beauty, all whose right
It is to work in sun and joy, who mean
To see the work they do and have it seen;
And when this plea starts rising up from the gloom,
I stretch my soul, to give the cry more room
To resonate and roll and amplify
And thus become an ever greater cry;
I hold it, like a prayer, within my soul
For just a moment; then, as I tense the whole
Of my being, gathering strength to hurl the song,
I'm positive my aim is true and strong;
My faith is absolute; I know my crow
Will tumble down the Night like Jericho. . .

                    PHEASANT
Chantecler!

                    CHANTECLER
                              And trumpeting its victory,
My song wells up, so clear and proud and peremptory
That all the East is seized with rosy trembling,
And it obeys me!

                    PHEASANT
                    Chantecler!

                    CHANTECLER
                                        I sing!

Night offers twilight, making a last appeal;
I sing! And suddenly. . .

                    PHEASANT
                    Chantecler!

CHANTECLER

I reel

Back in a crimson flod, my feathers run;
I see that I, the Cock, have raised the Sun!

PHEASANT

Your secret, then...?

CHANTECLER
Is that I dare to fear
The East would lie asleep without my song.
I do not sing to hear the echo flatter
Me; I think of light, and not of glory.
Singing, that's my way of fighting and holding
Up my beliefs; and if my song is the proudest
One of all, the reason is that I
Sing clearly so that it shall be clear!

PHEASANT

It's mad.

You think you bring to birth...?

CHANTECLER
Yes, that which opens
Up the bud, the eye, the soul, the window.
Certainly! My voice dispenses the light.
And gray skies mean I wasn't singing right.

PHEASANT
But don't you sing in broad daylight?

CHANTECLER
For practice.
Or, I'm telling all the tools on the farm
That I will do my duty and be their alarm.

PHEASANT
Who wakes you, then?

CHANTECLER
The fear that I'll forget.

PHEASANT
And you believe your voice can flood the world?

CHANTECLER, *simply*
I don't know very much about the world.
I sing for my own valley, hoping every
Valley has a cock who does the same.

PHEASANT

However. . .

CHANTECLER
Here I'm making speeches, when
I should be thinking how to make my dawn.

PHEASANT

His dawn?

CHANTECLER
You think it's madness? I will make
The Dawn arise before your very eyes!
I want to please you, and that desire is adding
Something new to my soul; I feel I'll sing
As if I stood upon the highest peak,
And Dawn will rise more beautifully than ever.

PHEASANT

More than ever?

CHANTECLER
Yes! Because a song
Grows even stronger knowing it is heard;
A deed is beter done for being seen.
        He plants himself on a hillock in the rear,
        overlooking the valley.
Madame!

PHEASANT
seeing him silhouetted against the sky
How handsome he is.

CHANTECLER
Watch the sky.
It's growing pale already? That's because
The song I sang just now commanded the sun
To stand in readiness below the rim.

PHEASANT
He looks so handsome he could even be right.

CHANTECLER
Sun! I feel you stirring over there!
My wattles shake; I laugh with pride already!

        And, rising erect on his spurs, he suddenly
        says in a piercing voice
Cock-a-doodle-doo!

PHEASANT
What gives him his strength?

CHANTECLER
Obey me! I am Earth and Labor! My crest
Is fire in the forge *couchant*, and the voice of the furrow
Rises up in my throat!
He whispers mysteriously:
Yes, yes, July?

PHEASANT
Whom is he talking to?

CHANTECLER
I'll see that yours
Come earlier than the month of April's did.
bending left and right, as if to reassure
Yes, Bush! Yes, Fern!

PHEASANT
Oh, he's magnificent.

CHANTECLER, *to the Pheasant*
I always have to think...
He caresses the ground with his wing.
Yes, Grass!
to the Pheasant
...Of all

The humble wishes that find a voice through me.
speaking again to invisible beings
A golden ladder?... Yes... to dance in a group.

PHEASANT
Who wants a ladder?

CHANTECLER
All the Motes of Dust.
—Cock-a-doodle-doo!

PHEASANT
A shiver of blue
Runs on the roofs. A star goes out.

CHANTECLER
No,
Pulls down her veil. Even when it's day
The stars are there.

PHEASANT
Don't you put them out?

CHANTECLER, *proudly*
I don't know how to put things out. But see
How I can set them on fire!

PHEASANT
Oh! the blue. . .

CHANTECLER
Yes?

PHEASANT
Is blue no longer.

CHANTECLER
Green already?

PHEASANT
Now it's turning amber!

CHANTECLER
You're the first
This morning who has seen that golden change.

The distant plain grows a velvety purple.

PHEASANT
The whole world seems to end in fields of heather.

CHANTECLER, *whose cry begins to tire*
Cock-a-. . .

PHEASANT
Look! There's yellow—down in the pines!

CHANTECLER
It must be gold!

PHEASANT
There's gray!

CHANTECLER
It must be white!
I haven't done it! Cock-a-doodle-doo!
It's looking bad! But then, I'm stubborn.

PHEASANT

Every

Hollow in every tree is glowing rose.

CHANTECLER, *with growing enthusiasm*
Since love has joined my faith today, I want
A day more beautiful that day itself.
Look! My voice has streaked the East with color!

PHEASANT, *swept along by the Cock's madness*
Maybe so, since love is helping him!

CHANTECLER
Horizon! When you hear my call, take up
Your ranks again, your rows of poplars!

PHEASANT, *bending over the valley*

Out

Of darkness comes a world that you create.

CHANTECLER
You're witnessing the birth of sacred things.
—You hills out there, your contours must be sharper!—
Pheasant, do you love me?

PHEASANT

We will always
Love to share the secret of Calling the Dawn.

CHANTECLER
You help my song. Come closer. Work with me.

PHEASANT, *springing to his side*
I love you!

CHANTECLER
Yes! The words you whisper here
Become the sunshine over there.

PHEASANT

I love you!

CHANTECLER
Say that you adore me—then I'll gild
That mountain with just one stroke.

PHEASANT, *beside herself*
Then I adore you!

CHANTECLER
sending forth his most brilliant cry

Cock-a-doodle-doo!

The mountain turns gold.

PHEASANT
pointing to the lower ranges that are still purple
The foothills too?

CHANTECLER
Each has its turn. The heights are first to feel
The touch of day. —Cock-a-doodle-doo!

PHEASANT
A golden ray has roused a sleeping hill.

CHANTECLER, *joyously*
Here! I dedicate that ray to you.

PHEASANT
The distant villages come into view.

CHANTECLER
Cock...

His voice breaks.

PHEASANT
You can't do any more.

CHANTECLER, *stiffening*
I must!

Cock-a-doodle-doo! Cock-a-doodle-
Doo!

PHEASANT
You're so exhausted.

CHANTECLER
Don't you see
Those shreds of gray? —Cock-a-doodle-doo!

PHEASANT
You'll kill yourself.

CHANTECLER
I only live when I
Can kill myself in giving greater cries!

PHEASANT, *pressed close to him*

I'm proud of you.

CHANTECLER, *moved*
You lean your head on me?

PHEASANT
I hear the new day rising up in your breast.
I love to hear it first within your lungs:
The power that will turn the mountains gold.

CHANTECLER
as the little houses in the distance begin
to send up smoke in the dawn
I dedicate those waking farms to you:
Where men give ribbons, I give plumes of smoke.

PHEASANT, *looking at the plain*
I see your work grow larger, there in the distance.

CHANTECLER, *looking at her*
I see it here, in your eyes.

PHEASANT
Out on the meadows.

CHANTECLER
Here on your throat.
suddenly, in a choking voice
It's wonderful!

PHEASANT
What is?

CHANTECLER
That doing my work has made you still more lovely:
While my valley turned gold, so did your wing.
But, tearing himself away from tender thoughts,
he dashes to the right.
The shadow's in retreat but still puts up
A fight. There's work to do over there! Cock-
A-doodle-doo!

PHEASANT, *watching the sky*
Oh, look!

CHANTECLER, *looks and says sadly*
What can I do?
The morning star is fading.

PHEASANT
with regret for the bright spark the Light must eclipse
Fading...

CHANTECLER
Ah...
But we can't be sad.
And, tearing himself away from melancholy thoughts,
he dashes to the left.
There's work to do over here.
Cock...
At this moment the song of the other cocks rises
from the valley. He stops and says softly
There. You hear them now?

PHEASANT
Who dares?

CHANTECLER
The other cocks.

PHEASANT, *bending over the plain*
They sing in the rosy light.

CHANTECLER
They believe in the light as soon as they can see it.

PHEASANT
They sing in the blue...

CHANTECLER
I sang when it was black.
My song was raised in shadow; it was first.
In darkness, that's when it's brave to believe in the light.

PHEASANT, *indignantly*
How dare they sing while you still sing?

CHANTECLER
No matter.
Joined with mine, their songs acquire a meaning;
Late, but strong in numbers, they all help
Unknowingly to hasten night's retreat.
Standing erect on his hillock, he calls
to the Cocks in the distance
Together now...

CHANTECLER AND ALL THE COCKS
Cock-a-doodle-doo!

CHANTECLER, *alone, in a familiar and cordial tone*
Day, have courage!

PHEASANT, *at his side, stamping her foot*
Courage!

CHANTECLER
calling out encouragement to the Light
Yes, you must put
Some gold on that roof over there! Some green on that field
Of hemp!

PHEASANT, *transported*
Some white on the road!

CHANTECLER
Some blue on the stream!

PHEASANT, *in a great cry*
The Sun! The Sun!

CHANTECLER
I see it! There it is!
But now we have to pull it out of the trees!
And both of them, pulling backwards together, seem to be heaving the
sun towards them. Chantecler prolongs his cry as if to haul the sun out with it.
Cock...

PHEASANT, *calling through Chantecler's song*
Here it comes!

CHANTECLER
...a...

PHEASANT
Here it is!

CHANTECLER
...doo...

PHEASANT
Rising up...

CHANTECLER
..dle...

PHEASANT
Climbing out...

CHANTECLER

...doo!

PHEASANT

...Of the elms!

CHANTECLER, *in a last, desperate cry*
Cock-a-doodle-doo!
> *The two of them stagger, suddenly flooded with light.*

At last! It's done!
> *with satisfaction*

It's huge.
> *He goes to a slope and falls against it, exhausted.*

PHEASANT
> *running to him, as everything grows bright*

A song to salute the beautiful sun.

CHANTECLER, *very low*
No. I have no voice. I gave it all.
> *And, as all the Cocks sing in the valley, he adds softly*

It doesn't matter. He has other fanfares.

PHEASANT, *surprised*
What! no songs from you when he appears?

CHANTECLER
No.

PHEASANT, *indignant*
But then perhaps he thinks it's they
Who made him rise?

CHANTECLER
It doesn't matter.

PHEASANT

But...

CHANTECLER
Sssh! Come here to my heart, so I may thank you.
Never has there been a better dawn.

PHEASANT
But then, what compensates you for your pains?

CHANTECLER

The sounds of life that start to rise from the valley.
And indeed, the clamor of life begins to rise.
Describe them. I don't have the strength to listen.

PHEASANT
who runs to lean over the rise and listen
A finger beats against a copper sky...

CHANTECLER, *eyes closed*

The Angelus.

PHEASANT
Smaller blows, as if
A human angelus would follow God's.

CHANTECLER

The forge.

PHEASANT
Mosquitoes buzz and swarm in a cloud...

CHANTECLER

The saw.

PHEASANT
A burst of tiny cries, as though
A nest had fallen down to the street.

CHANTECLER, *with growing emotion*

The school!

PHEASANT
A hundred puppies panting fast...

CHANTECLER

The train!

PHEASANT
And all at once, on every side, what are
Those iron beetles clicking iron legs?

CHANTECLER, *erect again, full of pride*
Ah! the harvest combines cut their golden
Passage through the wheat!
*The noises grow and mingle: bells, hammers,
saws, motors, laughter, shouting.*
They're all at work.
And I did that!... Impossible! Pheasant,

Help me, now I face the dreadful moment.
He looks around him distractedly.
I have made the sun rise. . . me! But why?
How? Where? The moment I regain
My reason, I go mad. For I, who think
I can rekindle all the gold of heaven. . .
Oh, it's horrible!

PHEASANT

What is?

CHANTECLER

I'm modest.

You won't tell?

PHEASANT
No, my love.

CHANTECLER

You swear?

Oh, that my enemies may never know. . .

PHEASANT, *moved*

Chantecler!

CHANTECLER
I feel I don't deserve
My glory. Why have I been chosen to be
The one who banishes night? Yes, as soon
As I have lit the incandescent sky,
The pride that sent me soaring hurls me down.
Can I, so small, have made the giant dawn?
And having done it, must I do it again?
I can't! I never will! I'm in despair!
Console me!

PHEASANT, *tenderly*

Darling!

CHANTECLER
So much rests on me.
The inspiration I seek when I scratch in the sand,
Will it return? I feel as if the future
Rests on some unknown that may desert me.
Now do you understand the pain I feel?
Ah, the swan who arcs his neck is certain
He will find sweet grasses down in the lake;
The eagle knows he plummets toward a victim;

You are sure the earth hold nests of ants;
But I, whose work remains a mystery,
Who know the terror of every tomorrow, can I
Be sure I'll find my song within my heart?

                    PHEASANT, *enfolding him with her wings*
Yes, you'll find it, yes.

                         CHANTECLER
                                  Tell me so.
I need those words. Believe in me when I
Believe, not when I doubt. Tell me again...

                         PHEASANT

You're handsome.

                         CHANTECLER
             I don't care.

                         PHEASANT
                                  You sang very well.

                         CHANTECLER
Say that I sang badly, but say that I
Can make the dawn...

                         PHEASANT
                    Yes, yes, how I admire you!

                         CHANTECLER
No! Tell me that what I said is true.

                         PHEASANT
What?

                         CHANTECLER
             Say that I'm the one who makes...

                         PHEASANT
Yes, my love, it's you who make the dawn.

                    BLACKBIRD, *appearing suddenly*
Well, old man!

                         CHANTECLER
                    The Blackbird!... Oh, my secret...

                    BLACKBIRD, *bowing in admiration*
Well!

CHANTECLER

That cynic!
to the Pheasant
Don't leave us alone.
My soul is open. All his gibes would enter.

BLACKBIRD

Beautiful!

CHANTECLER
But where did you come from?

BLACKBIRD
indicating an empty, overturned flower pot

That pot.

CHANTECLER

But how?

BLACKBIRD
I sat inside the terra
Cotta, snacking away on a raw earwig,
When all at once... Let me tell you
Instantly how dazzled...

CHANTECLER
But...

BLACKBIRD
But what? You didn't
Know that little pots could have big ears?

CHANTECLER
Eavesdropping in a pot! How could you stoop to that?

BLACKBIRD
Forget the pot! Who cares, when one is drunk?
And I was drunk! The greatest! I was wild!
I stamped on the clay and gaped through the hole!

PHEASANT

You saw?

BLACKBIRD
indicating the hole at the bottom of the pot
Of course. That cone of red has a nice black hole
That fits my yellow beak. And what a sight!
Forgive me, but you know that I have taste.

PHEASANT

Since you admire him, I forgive it all.

CHANTECLER

But what...

BLACKBIRD

The gorgeous beauty of it!... Lord,
I'm going pleonastic.

CHANTECLER, *astonished*

What! Can you—

BLACKBIRD

Enthusiasm's not my sport, you know,
But this time, old man, I was in a Transport.

CHANTECLER

Really?

BLACKBIRD

When I admire you, I don't wait
To send the news by carrier pigeon. The Cock
Who sings, bravo! The dawn that breaks, bravo!

PHEASANT, *to the Cock*

I think that I can leave you with him now.

CHANTECLER

Where will you go?

PHEASANT, *a little ashamed of her frivolity*

I'm going to go...

BLACKBIRD

His song

Has even brought the Day... of the Guinea Hen.

CHANTECLER, *to the Pheasant*

Must I go too?

PHEASANT

You've reached such heights today

That I excuse you.

CHANTECLER, *with a touch of sadness*

But you are going to go?

PHEASANT, *gaily*
I have to show your sunlight play on my gown.
But I'll be back. Stay here.

BLACKBIRD
Yes, it's better
For him to stay away.

CHANTECLER, *looking at him*
Why?

BLACKBIRD, *quickly*
No reason.

falling into fresh ecstasies
Oh, this Rooster!

CHANTECLER, *to the Pheasant*
You'll come back soon?

PHEASANT
Yes, yes.

softly, before she leaves
You see, you've dazzled even the blackest of birds.

She flies off.

CHANTECLER
running to the Blackbird with abandon
Where's your mocking whistle?

BLACKBIRD
Silenced by a slap
In the face. I'm whistling now in admiration.
This way.
He whistles admiringly.
Whew!... Whew!...
nodding gravely
Wonderful!

CHANTECLER, *naively*
You're not so bad. I told the Dog.

BLACKBIRD, *with profound conviction*
It's great!

CHANTECLER, *modestly*
Oh, well...

BLACKBIRD
To charm the hens...
He whistles again admiringly.
Whew!... By making
Them believe you bring the dawn!
Chantecler starts.
Sounds easy?
Yes, but someone had to dream it up.
Oh, you weren't hatched out yesterday!

CHANTECLER
But you...

BLACKBIRD
Don Juan was just an ass compared to you:
The day's produced so hens can be seduced.
And it works!

CHANTECLER, *heavily*
Be quiet!

BLACKBIRD
Neat, that roof that must
Be gold! Superb, those motes of Dust!

CHANTECLER, *in a spasm of pain*
Be quiet!

BLACKBIRD
Then that fit of modesty... I love you!
Yes, he knows, all right!

CHANTECLER, *restraining himself*
Knows whom? The Dawn?
I have the honor to know her.

BLACKBIRD
Troubadour!
You can't believe you made it?

CHANTECLER
What? The Day?
Of course I made it. Here it is. It's lovely.

BLACKBIRD
Yes, my prophet, you pulled it off very well.

CHANTECLER
The Sun? Of course I'm used to pulling him up.
And he obeys me.

BLACKBIRD
Yes, my Joshua!
You feel the dawn is coming and then you sing.
There's never been a sharper lyric.

CHANTECLER
Wretch!

BLACKBIRD, *surprised*
You keep it up in front of me?
winking
But we
Know how it's done.

CHANTECLER
You do. Not I. I open
Up my heart and sing.

BLACKBIRD, *hopping*
Some system.

CHANTECLER
Mock
At everything, but if you love me, not
At that.

BLACKBIRD
Sure I love you.

CHANTECLER, *bitterly*
With half a heart.

BLACKBIRD
You think that when I kid your "Fiat Lux"
I'm just a half a Castor to your Pollux?

CHANTECLER
No, not that.

BLACKBIRD
Old man, it's not my fault:
I just don't kneel.

CHANTECLER, *watching him*
No, he hops, he hops!

and, trying to stop him
You see the state I'm in, don't dodge the issue!

BLACKBIRD, *hopping past*
Catch the Artful Dodger!

CHANTECLER, *pleading*
This involves
My life, my deepest feelings! Oh, I must
Convince you, be it only for a moment.
I must reach your soul...

BLACKBIRD, *hopping past*
Ah, yes?

CHANTECLER
Just once.

At heart you do believe me, don't you?

BLACKBIRD
Sure.

CHANTECLER, *with the most pressing anguish*
I think you know what price I pay for my song?

BLACKBIRD
I do?

CHANTECLER
You hear me, don't you?

BLACKBIRD
Well, I listen.

CHANTECLER
Look, to sing the way I do, you know
Very well that one must be—

BLACKBIRD
In perfect health.

CHANTECLER
Ah, let's be serious, because we both
Have wings!

BLACKBIRD
Yes, let's talk philosophy.

CHANTECLER
In order to see the dawn obey his cries,
One must have—

BLACKBIRD
Iron lungs and eagle eyes.

He hops out of the way.

CHANTECLER
This soul...
      controlling himself
            I must pursue him!
                  and, with a desperate patience
                        Don't you know
What the Dawn is?

BLACKBIRD
Sure, old man. It's when the East
—If I dare to put it this way—is in the pink.

He hops out of the way.

CHANTECLER
What do you say when you see the mountain glow
With dawn?

BLACKBIRD, *hopping out of the way*
I say the sun has called its bluff.

CHANTECLER, *following him*
What do you say when I sing in the furrow, long
Before the cricket?

BLACKBIRD
I say that's not cricket.

He hops out of the way.

CHANTECLER, *beside himself*
You've never felt the need to cry out something
When I've made a dawn so flaming red
That a distant ibis looks just like flamingo?

BLACKBIRD
Yes, old man, I almost cry out, "Bingo!"

CHANTECLER, *exhausted*
Oh, this soul... It's more exhausting chasing
Him than hunting grasshoppers all day long.

violently
Didn't you see the sky?

                    BLACKBIRD, *ingenuously*
                         I couldn't; through
That little black hole you only see the ground.

                    CHANTECLER
Didn't you see the trembling heights turn scarlet?

                    BLACKBIRD
Whie you were singing I watched your feet.

                    CHANTECLER, *sadly*
                                                        Ah.

                    BLACKBIRD
They hit the sod in a new routine, the daybreak
Buck and wing.

                    CHANTECLER, *giving up*
                         I pity you. Go back
To your blackness.

                    BLACKBIRD
              Yes, o celebrated Cock.

                    CHANTECLER
I head for the sun.

                    BLACKBIRD
                    Be sure you wear dark glasses.

                    CHANTECLER
Don't you know the only thing that makes
A life worth living?

                    BLACKBIRD
                    No debates now, please.

                    CHANTECLER
It's Effort! that which makes the lowest creature
Sacred! You who sneer at aspiration,
That's why I despise you. But this fragile,
Rosy snail, who tries all by himself
To coat that stick with silver, him I admire.

BLACKBIRD

Oh, I can swallow that.

He quickly gulps down the snail.

CHANTECLER
It's infamous!

You snuff out a tiny flame to make a pun!
There's no more heart in you than soul. We're through.

BLACKBIRD, *hopping on a pile of sticks*

But I have brains.

CHANTECLER, *turning, contemptuously*
That's an open question.

BLACKBIRD, *becoming acid*

All right, then. I offered you some grains
Of sense, but now I wash my claws of you.
Go do just what your enemies are saying.

CHANTECLER, *going to him*

Who? and what?

BLACKBIRD
Go play you're God and cry,

"Let there be light!"

CHANTECLER
You're friends with those who hate me?

BLACKBIRD

That annoys you?

CHANTECLER
No, poor clown. The habit

Has grown too strong; you couldn't stop the sneering
Now if you wanted, even with your friends.
    marching on him
Who are my enemies?

BLACKBIRD
The Owls.

CHANTECLER

You fool.

It's easy to believe I bring the light if they're
The ones who hate me.

BLACKBIRD
Then be happy: since
They find the light too harsh, the plan to cut...

CHANTECLER

Well, what?

BLACKBIRD

The current.

CHANTECLER
What?

BLACKBIRD

Your throat.

CHANTECLER

Who does?

BLACKBIRD

A brother bird.

CHANTECLER
A Cock?

BLACKBIRD

A real Saint George!

Who's set to meet you...

CHANTECLER
Where?

BLACKBIRD

At the Guinea Hen's.

CHANTECLER

Bah!

BLACKBIRD
He's bred for combat, one of those Cocks
Who'd make a hash of us if we showed up...
seeing Chantecler abruptly start toward the rear
Where are you going?

CHANTECLER
Off to the Guinea Hen's.

BLACKBIRD
Oh yes, that's right, I forgot his shining armor.
He makes a feint at stopping Chantecler.
No, don't go.

CHANTECLER
I will.

BLACKBIRD
No, don't.

CHANTECLER
stopping in front of the pot, struck by a thought.
Hold on.

BLACKBIRD
What now?

CHANTECLER
You weren't inside this flower pot?

BLACKBIRD
Of course.

CHANTECLER, *incredulous*
But how?

BLACKBIRD, *quickly re-entering the pot*
I'll say it once again:
He sticks his beak out of the hole at the bottom.
Through this little black hole I looked—

CHANTECLER

At the ground?

Well, here's a little blue hole to look at the sky!
And with a formidable blow of his wing he turns
the pot over the Blackbird, who is heard fluttering
beneath his clay hat, with smothered whistles.
You Pot-Bound creatures hide from the blue, but sometimes
One can force your eye to a patch of sky
By tipping up the pots that cramp your souls!

He exits.

The curtain falls.

ACT THREE

The Day of the Guinea Hen

THE SCENE: A corner of the garden.

Vegetables and flowers. Eggplant and lily. A bouquet for the Nymph and a meal for the Faun. A rose, reigning from a pumpkin throne. Lavender for the sachet. Onions for the stew.

Thrusting up from the big cabbages and turning its black face with yellow collar toward the god whose alms it seeks, the sunflower acquires a stiff green neck.

The scarecrow is silhouetted among the berry bushes. A watering can can be seen, near a wheelbarrow. A spade is planted among the artichokes.

A little white wall covers one whole side; and a strawberry, casting its shadow against the whitewash, seems to be a blackberry.

AT RISE: a great stirring and jabbering of HENS and CHICKENS; THE GUINEA HEN rushing among them; AN INVISIBLE CHOIR OF WASPS, BEES, and CICADAS.

GUINEA HEN
going impetuously from one to another
Hello, hello! — What a crush! So many came
That my crowd goes all the way to the cucumber frame.

A CHOIR, *in the air*
We hum and buzz . . .

GUINEA HEN, *to a Hen*
Just one of my little affairs.

A HEN
looking at some huge pumpkins, like stoneware
How nice.

GUINEA HEN
A touch of art. Ceramics.

A CHICK, *beak lifted, listening to the choir*
Singers?

GUINEA HEN
Yes.

CHOIR
We buzz and hum . . .

GUINEA HEN, *brightly*
The Wasps!
to a Chick
Hello!
She flits away.

WASP CHOIR
We throng...among...the berries...honey-tongued...

PHEASANT
passing by with the Blackbird, laughing
So you were caught?

BLACKBIRD, *finishing his tale*
As if beneath a hat.
But I thrashed about and turned the pot upright.
looking around
So Chantecler's not here?

PHEASANT
He's coming, then?

PATOU
*appearing suddenly on the wheelbarrow, from which
he watches the coming and going, as if at a rostrum*
I'm hoping he'll still change his mind.

BLACKBIRD
Patou?
In a barrow?

PATOU, *shaking his surly head; a bit of
broken chain hangs from his collar*
Chantecler passed by my house
And told me all. I broke my chain in a rage
And came to see.

GUINEA HEN, *seeing the Blackbird*
He's here? That good-for-nothing
In a seedy old black coat?

A CHOIR, *in the trees*
Salute... the Sun...

PHEASANT, *lifting her head*
A choir?

GUINEA HEN
Yes, I have the Cicadas.

CICADA CHOIR
Sing...

A psalm... to bless you...

GUINEA COCK, *quickly, aside to his mother*
Say sicadas, Mother!

"Sic," not "chic."

A MAGPIE, *in black coat and white tie, announcing the guests
as they come in through one of those round holes
chickens dig at the feet of hedges*
The Gander!

THE GANDER, *entering, jocularly*
Say! We're announced?

GUINEA HEN, *modestly*
I hired an usher to stand at the blackberry gate.

MAGPIE, *announcing*

The Duck!

DUCK, *entering, astonished*
Oh! We're announced?

GUINEA HEN, *modestly*
Oh, yes. I hired—

MAGPIE

The Turkey Hen!

TURKEY HEN, *affectedly*
My, my. We're announced?

GUINEA HEN
Oh, yes.

I took the Magpie's husband on part-time.

CHOIR, *in some blossoming branches*
Our furry... feet...

TURKEY HEN, *lifting her beak*
A choir?

GUINEA HEN, *brightly*
I have the Bees!

BEE CHORUS

Are full. . . of pollen. . .

TURKEY HEN
Wonders everywhere!

GUINEA HEN
On one side, Bees; Cicadas on the other.
to a passing Hen
Hello!

BEES, *at the right*

Pollen. . .

CICADAS, *at the left*
Bless you. . .

BEES

Pollen. . .

CICADAS

Bless you!

GUINEA HEN, *to the Pheasant*
Yes, my garden holds the pick of the crop.

GUINEA COCK
Every guest is a peach.

GUINEA HEN
A plum!

BLACKBIRD

A lemon.

PHEASANT
jostled by the crowd; to the Blackbird
Let's find some room, behind this watering can.

BLACKBIRD
The watering can, nicknamed "Rapunzel": When
She leans, she lowers a shower of silver hair.

GUINEA HEN
*seeing the Cat, who is stretched on the branch
of an apple tree, watching everything*
I have the Cat!

BLACKBIRD
Who's nicknamed "Oedipuss Rex."

Whistling is heard in a tree.

GUINEA HEN, *leaping toward it*

I have the Lark!

BLACKBIRD
Not *Joan* of Lark?

PATOU, *disgusted*

Those puns!

GUINEA HEN

The Dragon-Fly!

BLACKBIRD
So thin he's "Peter Pin."

PATOU, *furious*

Witless bird!

GUINEA HEN
pecking a cabbage leaf, from which fall some drops of dew
I have the Dew!

PATOU, *snapping*

Does she

Have a nickname?

BLACKBIRD
"Pearls upon the grass, alas."

GUINEA HEN
pointing to several of the circulating Chicks
You saw? I've got the A. I. Chicks.

PHEASANT

A. I.?

GUINEA HEN

The Artificial Incubator.

presenting them

All

Top-drawer, you see.

PHEASANT
They are?

A CHICK, *nudging his neighbor*
                              She's thunderstruck.

                    GUINEA HEN, *contemptuously*
Eggs one hatches...

                        BLACKBIRD
                    They're beneath you, eh?

                    MAGPIE, *announcing*
The Guinea Pig!

                        GUINEA HEN
                    Of the famous family.
You know, from the laboratories. Yes, I have him.
I have everyone. I have...
                    to the Guinea Pig
                                              Hello!

        to the Pheasant
...Our great philosopher, the Turkey, who
Will give a talk by the currant bush...
                            to a passing Hen
                                              Hello!

        to the Pheasant
...a Lecture, I should say, on Currant Affairs.
        She whirls about.
I have them all! I have the golden Pheasant!
I have the Duck, who'll organize some games.
I have the Turtle...
            realizing he is not there
                        No! I don't! He's late!

                        BLACKBIRD
What's this lecture about, that he's going to miss?

                    GUINEA HEN, *gravely*
The Moral Crisis.

                    BLACKBIRD, *desolated*
                        Oh!

            The Guinea Hen darts away.

            PHEASANT, *to the Blackbird*
                        Who is this Turtle?

> BLACKBIRD

A tough old type in loud check suits who's deaf
To moral crises.

> *There is a buzzing in the hollyhocks.*

> PHEASANT
> Look! A bumblebee!

> GUINEA HEN, *rushing back to them*

I have the Bumblebee! How chic he is,
In the light!

> BLACKBIRD
> That's bumbling at its height.

> GUINEA HEN, *hopping up toward the Bumblebee*
>   Hello!

> *She whirls after him.*

> BLACKBIRD, *touching his wing to his brow*

She's batty.

> GUINEA HEN, *shrieking at the rear*
> It's my last affair of the month! —

Hello! —My big goodbye to July!

> A HEN, *seeing cherries fall around her*
>   Oh, look!

Cherries...

> PHEASANT, *lifting her head*
> I think it's the breeze.

> GUINEA HEN, *rushing back*
>   I have the Breeze!

She sends a cherry now and then. You can't
Invite her—she just comes. I have the... Yes,
I have... I have...

> *She darts away.*

> BLACKBIRD
>   Oh, when will she have *had* it?

*Hopping along, he has arrived at the tree where
the Cat lies. Quickly, under his breath*

Cat—the plot?

CAT
from his branch, looking over the hedge
It's on. Here comes a file
Of those exotic Cocks the Peacock calls
The avant-garde.

A CRY, *outside*
Eee-yong!

PATOU, *grumbling*
That voice. . .

MAGPIE USHER, *announcing*
The Peacock!

PHEASANT, *to the Blackbird*
Nicknamed what?

BLACKBIRD
The Shriek of Araby.

GUINEA HEN
as the Peacock enters slowly, head high and stiff
Master, dear! Right here—by the sunflowers! Oh. . .
Peacock, sunflowers—it's all so Art Nouveau.

ALL, *crowding around him*
Dear Master!

A CHICKEN, *to a Duck*
Just one word from him, and you're made.

ANOTHER CHICKEN
who has pushed his way to the Peacock,
stammering with emotion
Dear Master, what do you think of my latest chirp?

A solemn wait.

PEACOCK
Phenomenal.

Sensation.

A DUCK, *trembling*
My quack?

A wait.

PEACOCK
Ineffable.

Sensation.

GUINEA HEN, *thrilled, to the Hens*
He's at his best at my affairs; his thoughts
Are so...

PEACOCK
Hebdomadal.

ALL THE HENS, *swooning*
Ah!

A HEN
coming forward, faint with emotion

Dear sacred

Maker of taste, what do you think of my dress?

A wait.

PEACOCK, *after a glance*

Acceptable.

Sensation.

SPECKLED HEN, *same business*
My hat?
A wait.

PEACOCK
Proportional.

GUINEA HEN, *wild*
Our hats are proportional!

PHEASANT
pretending to listen only to the Bees
The choir is back.

GUINEA HEN
presenting the Guinea Cock to the Peacock
And what do you think of my son?

PEACOCK
Plausible.

BEE CHOIR
We hum... and thrum...

GUINEA HEN, *thrilled, rushing to the Pheasant*
He's plausible!

PHEASANT

Who is?

GUINEA HEN

My son!

BEE CHOIR
We hum... and thrum... among... the mums...

GUINEA HEN, *to the Peacock*
The choir's rhythm, don't you think that it's...

PEACOCK

Iambic.

A HEN, *to the Guinea Hen*
There, my dear, is an epithet.

GUINEA HEN
He's Prince of the Unexpected Adjective.

PEACOCK
layng out each word, in a haughty, discordant voice
True it is that I...

GUINEA HEN
He's speaking!

PEACOCK

...A Ruskin

More refined, with sensitivity...

GUINEA HEN

Oh, yes!

PEACOCK
...for which I can credit only myself,
Serve as Petronius-Priest and Maecenas-Messiah,
A volatile volatiliser of words;
And that, a jeweled judge, I love, from my
Prismatic perch, to represent that Taste
Of which I am...

PATOU
My head aches.

PEACOCK, *nonchalantly*
Shall I say,

The guardian?

GUINEA HEN, *excitedly*

Yes!

PEACOCK

No. The Justinian, I think.

Murmurs of respectful pleasure.

GUINEA HEN, *to the Pheasant*

So, you've seen our Peacock. Aren't you thrilled?

PHEASANT

Oh, yes, because I know the Cock is coming.

GUINEA HEN, *delighted*

Here? Today? Why, then my little affair
Will be...

PEACOCK, *dryly*

A spectacle.

GUINEA HEN

Spectacular!

She announces enthusiastically to everyone.

Chantecler!

PEACOCK, *low*
You'll have an even greater

Triumph.

GUINEA HEN

Triumph?
The Peacock nods mysteriously.
What?

PEACOCK, *moving away*
You'll see.

GUINEA HEN, *following him*

But what?

MAGPIE USHER, *announcing*

The Braekel or Campine Cock!

GUINEA HEN, *stopping, astounded*
A Braekel? Here?

There must be some mistake.

BRAEKEL COCK, *bowing to her*
Madame.

GUINEA HEN
breathless before this white cock with black braiding

I'm stunned...

MAGPIE, *announcing*
The Ramelsloh Cock with a slate-blue claw!

GUINEA HEN

Oh, Lord!

MAGPIE
The Wyandotte with sable spurs!

The Hens shiver with emotion.

GUINEA HEN, *distractedly*

Oh, heavens...

Lord... Oh, son!

GUINEA COCK, *running to her*
Mama!

GUINEA HEN
A Wyandotte!

PEACOCK, *carelessly*
Whose rose comb shows the influence—does it not?—
Of minimalism.

GUINEA HEN
to the newcomers, surrounded by murmurs of amazement
Rose comb... Mini... Oh, sirs...

GUINEA COCK, *looking outside*
Mama!

GUINEA HEN
At my affair...

GUINEA COCK
More are coming!

MAGPIE
Cock of...

GUINEA HEN
Heavens! Of what?

MAGPIE
                          The Cock of Iraq,
With a double comb!

GUINEA HEN
It's double?
                    rushing to the newcomer
                          Sir! dear sir!

PEACOCK
We must have done with obscolescent forms.
I wished to show you several young Messieurs
Whose splendid shapes embody recent trends.

GUINEA HEN, *going back to the Peacock*
Oh, thank you, Peacock.
               to the Pheasant, patronizingly
                          Dear, you must excuse me,
But, you see, the Iraqi Cock has come
To see me.
          She rushes to him; he inclines his double comb.
                    We're so proud to have you here.

MAGPIE
The Orpington, with feathers ringing the eye!

GUINEA HEN
Ringing... no...

BLACKBIRD
She's ding-a-linging.

GUINEA HEN
                                          Oh...

MAGPIE
          as the Guinea Hen flies to the Orpington
The Bearded Cock of Varna!

PEACOCK, *to the Guinea Hen*
                          Very Slavic.

GUINEA HEN
          leaving the Orpington for the Bearded Varna
Yes, the Slavic soul... dear sir... oh, dear...

MAGPIE
The Scotch Gray with a pink foot!

GUINEA HEN
Pink! But I
Love pink! Oh, to launch a pink foot—what a coup!

MAGPIE
The Cock...

GUINEA HEN
Don't tell me there are more of them!

MAGPIE
...with a goblet comb!

GUINEA HEN
who flings herself enthusiastically at each newcomer
So new... a goblet... Sir!

MAGPIE
The Blue Andalusian Cock!

GUINEA HEN, *running to him*
They must have laid
Your egg in the vibrating hollow of a guitar.

MAGPIE
The Langshan Cock!

PEACOCK
A Tartar.

ALL THE HENS, *dazzled by this black giant*
Oh, a Tartar!

MAGPIE
Golden-Pencilled Hamburg Cock!

THE HENS
seeing this gold-laced Cock, topped with a tricorn
He's golden-
Pencilled! He's a Hamburg!

BLACKBIRD
Rare, with mustard.

GUINEA HEN
This little party of mine will be renowned.
*to the Hamburg, whose breast is
striped with yellow and black*
Oh, sir, your vest—what's it made of?

BLACKBIRD

                                             Zebra.

GUINEA HEN
Zebra! Nothing in my life will ever
Equal this!

MAGPIE
The Cock...

GUINEA HEN
                          Oh, no...

MAGPIE

                                             Of Burma!

GUINEA HEN
Burma!

The agitation grows.

PEACOCK
Indian, you know.

GUINEA HEN
                                             I see
The Hindu soul in his eyes.
She rushes to the newcomer; in an idolizing voice
                          Your soul! So Hindu!

MAGPIE
Polish Cocks—The Dutch Padua!

GUINEA HEN
                                             The Dutch
Of Poland... more than I ever dreamed.

The Polish Cocks enter, shaking their plumes.

MAGPIE
                                             The Golden!
The Bearded Silver!

GUINEA HEN
seeing the plumes cascading from the latter's head
                          Topped by a waterfall!

BLACKBIRD
With several bridges.

GUINEA HEN
Several bridges!

PHEASANT, *to Patou*

Now

She's just an echo.

MAGPIE
*announcing the more and more extraordinary Cocks
in a more and more piercing voice*
The Bantam Cock with ruffles!

GUINEA HEN
Oh, how eighteenth-century! A dwarf!
A dwarf! It's dwarfs!

GUINEA COCK, *low*
Mama, control yourself.

GUINEA HEN, *shrieking amidst the Cocks*
I can't. I don't know which one I prefer. . .

MAGPIE
The malay Cock with a serpent neck!

GUINEA HEN, *rattled, to the Peacock*

Oh, Seacock

Dear, we owe this perpent-neck to you. . .

MAGPIE
The duck-winged Cock! The crow-beak Cock! The Cock
With vulture hocks!

GUINEA HEN
rushing to the new arrivals and shrieking at the latter
Amazing. . . an albino!
Sir!. . . Look, on his head there's a cheese!

A HEN

A cream cheese!

ALL THE HENS

Cream cheese!

MAGPIE
Crève-coeur Cock!

GUINEA HEN, *rushing to him*
With horns on his head!

PEACOCK

Satanic.

MAGPIE

Ptarmigan Cock!

PEACOCK

Aesthetic.

GUINEA HEN

Look,

On his head—an Assyrian helmet!

MAGPIE

White Pile Cock!

GUINEA HEN, *rushing to him*

Look, on his head—
stopping short as she sees his clipped comb
There's nothing. Wonderful!

CAT
from the height of his apple tree, to the Blackbird
That's the duellist. His lean foot hides
A razor under the dust.

*The White Pile disappears in the crowd of exotic Cocks,
who are enveloped by shrieking Hens.*

MAGPIE

The Negro Cock!

GUINEA HEN
*wild in the midst of all these Cocks, who now fill
the garden with feathers, plumes, shakos, double
and triple combs*

Dear Sir!— Dear Sir!—

PATOU
She's lost her mind.

GUINEA HEN, *into thin air*

Dear Sir!

MAGPIE
The Cock with an extra toe! The Bare-Necked Cock!

GUINEA HEN

Bare-naked?

MAGPIE, *correcting*

Necked.

GUINEA HEN, *to a Hen*
My dear, a cock without

A collar!

MAGPIE
Japanese Cocks—the Yokohama!

GUINEA HEN
seeing that his tail is eight yards long
What an incredible train!

MAGPIE

The Speckled Quail Bantam.

BLACKBIRD
seeing that he's completely flat in the rear
That one's been derailed.

MAGPIE

...or Rumpless Cock!

GUINEA HEN, *beside herself*
He has no rear! It's the crowning of my whole career!
to the newcomer, effusively:
Oh, sir! You're rumpless! That's... why, that's...

BLACKBIRD

That's cheeky.

MAGPIE

Blue Java! White Java!

BLACKBIRD, *losing all shame*
Java see a dream walking?

GUINEA HEN, *rushing to the Javas*
Gentlemen... oh...

MAGPIE
The Brahma Cock! The Cochin!

PEACOCK, *haughtily*
All the great vicious Cocks—the corrupt Far East.

GUINEA HEN, *intoxicated*
Corrupt!

PEACOCK
Unwholesome charm.

GUINEA HEN, *to the Cochin*
Oh, sir, what an honor...
Oh, what an obscene eye!

MAGPIE
shouting wildly, as if seized by the general delirium
Frizzles from Chile—
With feathers curled forward! From Antwerp—feathers curled back!

ALL THE HENS, *breaking away to the newcomers*
Corrupt! Unwholesome!

GUINEA HEN
Forward!

MAGPIE
Footless Jumping
Cock!

A HEN, *swooning*
He jumps on his stomach!

PHEASANT
to Patou, who from his barrow searches the distance
And Chantecler?

PATOU
Soon.

PHEASANT
You see him?

PATOU
Over there, scratching
The earth. He's coming.

MAGPIE
The Cock with a parasol comb!

EXCITED CRIES
Oh! Ah!

MAGPIE
The white-faced Black Spanish Cock!

CRIES
Oh! Ah!

MAGPIE

The Bearded Thuringian!

CRIES
Oh! Ah!

MAGPIE
The barred Plymouth Rock!

CHANTECLER
appearing on the threshold, behind the latter
Announce me, please, as just the Cock.

MAGPIE, *sizes him up; then disdainfully:*
The Cock!

CHANTECLER
from the threshold, to the Guinea Hen, bowing
Forgive me, Madame, for daring to come in plumage
Like this...

GUINEA HEN
Come in!

CHANTECLER
I don't know whether I should.
I have, you see, a limited number of toes.

GUINEA HEN, *indulgently*
No matter.

CHANTECLER
I claim no Eastern ancestry,
And... there's no way to hide it... I have feet.
My comb's a pimento, my ear a clove of garlic...

GUINEA HEN
You're forgiven. You came in working clothes.

CHANTECLER, *moving in*
For a suit I've only—excuse my being so sober—
The green of April and the gold of October. I'm
Ashamed. I am the Cock, just the Cock,
That one still finds sometimes in an old farmyard,
A rooster shaped like a rooster, one whose form
Remains on steeple vanes, in an artist's eye,
In a toy a child's hand pulls from a candy box.

A VOICE, *ironic, from the dazzled group*
The simple native Cock?

CHANTECLER, *gently, without turning around*
When you're as sure
As I that the soil contains your roots, you'd never
Use those words; but now you mention it,
I see that's what one means by 'just the Cock.'

BLACKBIRD, *low, to Chantecler*
I've seen your killer.

CHANTECLER
who sees the Pheasant approaching
Ssh! She's not to know
A thing.

PHEASANT
You came to see me?

CHANTECLER, *bowing*
I gave in.

GUINEA HEN
as the Cochin, surrounded by Hens, whispers to them
The Chinese Cochin Cock... the way he talks!

CHANTECLER, *turning around*
Enough of that.

THE HENS, *uttering scandalized little cries*
Oh, my!

GUINEA HEN, *enchanted*
Our most salacious
Gallinacean.

CHANTECLER, *louder*
That's enough of that!

COCHIN, *stops, and with mocking surprise:*
The simple native Cock?

CHANTECLER
Not simple, in
The way you're trying to twist that word. Good Lord,
The hens all know my crow is not soprano.

But to tell them risqué tales in corners,
Just so one can pinch their parson's-noses. . .
That revolts my love of Love! I want
A cleaner passion than those Cochin Cocks,
Who make elaborate jokes about the mud
They love to roll around in. My blood runs
More quickly in a body that's not so gross as theirs;
For I'm not a pig, but a Cock.

> PHEASANT, *low, to him*
>   Come with me
> To the woods. I love you.

> CHANTECLER, *looking around him*
>   Oh, to see a being
> Who's simple and real. . .

> MAGPIE, *announcing*
>   The Pigeons!

> CHANTECLER, *to the Guinea Hen*
>   Really?

> GUINEA HENS
>   Yes.

> TWO PIGEONS, *entering, with perilous leaps*
> Hola!

> CHANTECLER, *recoiling*
>   They're acrobats.

> PIGEONS
> *introducing themselves, between somersaults*
>   Russian clowns!

> GUINEA HEN
> *bounding after them as they lose themselves in the crowd of guests*
> Hola! Hola!

> CHANTECLER
>   Pigeons turning tumblers!
> Oh, for something true. . .

> MAGPIE
>   The Swan!

> CHANTECLER, *advances eagerly but pulls back*
>   He's black!

SWAN, *strutting with satisfaction*
I dropped the whiteness, you see, but I kept the line.

CHANTECLER
You're just the real swan's shadow.
*Pushes him aside and hops on a bench from which, through
a gap in the hedge, he can see the meadow in the distance.*
Let me climb
This bench. I need to see if Nature still
Exists... out there. Ah yes, the grass is green,
And there's a grazing cow, a suckling calf.
Heaven be praised, the calf has just one head.
He climbs down, near the Pheasant.

PHEASANT
Come to the woods, where everything is fresh
And innocent and we can love each other.

BLACKBIRD
*to the Guinea Hen, indicating Chantecler and the
Pheasant as they speak together intimately*
They mean business, eh?

GUINEA HEN, *exhilarated*
You really think so?
opens her wings, to screen them
Oh, I love to be in on a secret affair.

BLACKBIRD
*putting his beak under the Guinea Hen's wing,
to follow the interplay*
I think she's planning to borrow his comb.

PHEASANT, *to Chantecler*
Come!

CHANTECLER, *pulling back in dismay*
I have to sing where fate has placed me. Here,
I'm useful and loved.

PHEASANT, *recalling what she heard in the barnyard at night*
You think so? No! Come
To the woods, where real creatures live and love.

TURKEY, *at the rear*
Mesdames, the great Peacock...

PEACOCK, *modestly*
                              The stupefying
Super-Peacock...

His tail!

TURKEY
                    ...will grant our pleas and spread

*The crowd forms into groups. All the exotic Cocks gather
around their patron like an ornamental basket holding flowers.*

PEACOCK, *preparing to spread his tail*
                This talent, plus my many others,
Makes me... shall I say, the fireworks artist?

GUINEA HEN

Yes!

PEACOCK
            No. The Pyrotechnist! For
The coruscating sparks that shower cities
Every Fourth of July, those amethyst
Capitula upon dodecagons
Of rockets, rank as far less sapphirine
Or cupric or smaragdine...

CHANTECLER
                              God in Heaven!

PEACOCK
...than, I dare to say, *mesdames*, am I...

PHEASANT
At last, a word I understood.

PEACOCK
                                        ...When I
Unfurl the faience-fan, the fretwork-firework...

ADMIRING CRY

Ah!

CHANTECLER, *to the Pheasant*
            The Goose!

PEACOCK
                ...on which I spread before
The rays that redden reeds, my joyous jewels.

CHANTECLER

The Prince of Fools!

The Peacock has spread his fan.

A COCK
Master, please, which
Of us will you declare to be the fashion?

A PADUA COCK, *coming forward*
I look like a palm tree!

A CHINESE COCK, *pushing the Padua aside*
I'm a pagoda!

A HUGE COCK WITH FEATHERERED LEGS
pushing the Chinese Cock aside
I have cauliflowers on my heels!

CHANTECLER
The Freak and P. T. Barnum rolled into one.

ALL, *parading and filing past the Peacock*
See my beak! — My feathers! — See my feet!

CHANTECLER, *suddenly shouting at them*
Look! The wind observes your beauty parade
And gives you all a Scarecrow's blessing!

*Indeed, behind them, the wind has lifted the arms of the
Scarecrow, which limply stretch out above the masquerade.*

ALL, *recoiling*
What?

CHANTECLER
And the Dummy speaks to the Fan!
*While the wind blows through the empty,
tattered rags, giving them a strange life:*
What say the pants
That dance a jig? Why... "I was once the rage."
What says that terror of the lark, the hat a bum
Would refuse to wear? Why... "I was once the rage."
The jacket? "I was once the rage!" The arms
No one would bother mending reach to seize
The wind, whose voice they take for fashion's voice...
And then fall back; the wind is gone!

PEACOCK
to the animals, who are a little frightened

Poor fools.

That Thing can't talk.

CHANTECLER
Man says that of us.

PEACOCK, *softly, to his neighbors*
The Cocks I introuded have made him angry.
to Chantecler, ironically
What do you think of all these splendid Cocks?

CHANTECLER
I think they were made by men with tortuous minds,
Who called it a feat of the intellect to make
A Chicken of the Absurd, taking a wing
From here and a wattle from there. I think there's nothing
Left in those cocks of a Rooster; they're all thrown
Together, pot-luck, made to guard a jar
Of cookies, not a barnyard. I think these twisted,
Frizzled, ganished cocks were never reared
And groomed by the calm maternal hand of Nature.
They're nothing but the tools of Aviculture.
I think these popinjays with jarring plumage,
Without style or line or grace, whose bodies
Don't even keep the lovely oval of the egg,
Were hatched in some Apocalyptic hen-house!

A COCK

Sir. . .

CHANTECLER
I say—and the Sun will say I'm right—
That a rooster's only duty is to be
A crimson cry! And if he isn't, he
Can puff and twist and turn his feathers inside
Out; he'll die achieving nothing but
A footnote in the Poultry Digest.

A COCK

Yes, but sir. . .

CHANTECLER
You Cocks who take uncockly shapes,
You Cockatrices, Shuttlecocks, and Mockeries
Of Cocks, all curled and coiffed with cocoa-palms. . .
My anger makes me talk like the Peacock, I

Alliterate... You cock-eyed Cockatoos,
You poppycocks with cockle-shell cockades,
Instead of crowing splendid cock-a-doodle-doos,
You Chicken Pox aspire to being
Laughing stocks! When Fashion says that freaks
Are chic, you click your claws, you Copy Cocks!
But no one keeps the crown of the king of freaks!
You're Cock for a Day, and then some other Cock
Appears with bigger ruffles on his coccyx!
Wait until tomorrow, Cockalorums!
Wait until the next day, Cock-a-hoops!
In spite of all your cock-brained quirks and tricks,
Some hen will hatch a still more cuckoo Cock
—Because, in order to vary his stock, the clever
Chicken Merchant cuckolds many Cocks—
And then you Capon-Cocks will be rococo
Rejects, next to that more freakish Cock:
Out-ranked, out-flanked, out-freaked, out-frocked, out-cocked!

A COCK
So how may we avoid a fate like that?

CHANTECLER
Think of nothing but your crowing.

A COCK, *haughtily*
Sir,

We do. We've made our crows well known.

CHANTECLER
To whom?

1st HOPPING CHICKEN
of three such, who have been circulating for a minute
or so among the artificial Cocks

To us!

2nd HOPPING CHICKEN
To us!

3rd HOPPING CHICKEN
To us!

ALL THREE, *bowing together*
Dear Sir.

1st CHICKEN
Your voice?

2nd CHICKEN
Is it bass?

3rd CHICKEN
Or tenor?

2nd CHICKEN
Pinza?

3rd CHICKEN
Pavarotti?

CHANTECLER, *bewildered, to the Guinea Hen*
What's this? An intermission?

GUINEA HEN
Interview.

2nd CHICKEN
Is it placed in your chest?

3rd CHICKEN
Your head?

CHANTECLER
Is *what* placed?

1st CHICKEN
Tell us!
We're investigating.

CHANTECLER, *trying to get away*
Investigating?

3rd CHICKEN, *barring the way*
The Cockadoodle Movement.

1st CHICKEN
Sir, is your
First meal a light one?

CHANTECLER
Who are you, whose questions
Poke like sticks?

1st CHICKEN, *bowing*
A Cockadoodle-ogue.

2nd CHICKEN, *bowing*
A Cockadoodle-ographer.

3rd CHICKEN

A Cock—

CHANTECLER

All right!

He tries to get by.

1st CHICKEN
No answers, then no getting away.

2nd CHICKEN
You must have certain preferences?

CHANTECLER, *surrounded*

Amen.

2nd CHICKEN
What do you find attracts you most?

CHANTECLER

A hen.

1st CHICKEN, *not amused*
You've nothing to say about your song?

CHANTECLER

I just...

Let it come.

2nd CHICKEN
And when you let it come?

CHANTECLER

It goes.

3rd CHICKEN, *more and more insistent*
What insecurities does it express?

CHANTECLER

But I...

1st CHICKEN

You live—

CHANTECLER
To sing!

2nd CHICKEN
And you sing?

CHANTECLER
                                                    To live.

3rd CHICKEN
Exactly *how* do you sing?

CHANTECLER
                                            By taking pains.

1st CHICKEN
But how do you scan? Cocka...doodle...doo?
Or Co...ckadoo...dledoo?

He beats the rhythm furiously with his wing.

CHANTECLER, *pulling back*
                                        He's going to hit me.

2nd CHICKEN
Please explain what scheme of dynamics you use.

BLACKBIRD
Everybody has one, you know.

CHANTECLER
                                                    Dyna...?

3rd CHICKEN
Where does the accent lie? On "Cock"?

CHANTECLER
                                            The accent...?

3rd CHICKEN
On "doo"?

1st CHICKEN, *impatiently*
                    What's your school?

CHANTECLER
                                        A school for Cocks...?

2nd CHICKEN
Yes, some use Cock-a-doodle-doo, but others—
Cawk-er-dewdle-dew.

3rd CHICKEN
                                        Not to mention...

                    A COCK, *coming forward*
The proper native crow is Ko-kay-ko-ko.

                         CHANTECLER
Who's that?

                         1st CHICKEN
          A Japanese.

                         2nd CHICKEN
                                   And over there,
That Turk whose comb looks like a cyst, he sings,
"Koo-kee-ah-koo."

                    ANOTHER COCK, *springing up on the right*
                         I suppress all the vowels.
K-k D-d D!

                    CHANTECLER, *trying to flee*
                              I must be dreaming.

          ANOTHER COCK, *advancing from the left, singing*
AH-ah OO-uh OO! Say, did you ever
Try suppressing the consonants?

                         CHANTECLER
                                        What have
They managed to do with five plain syllables?

               ANOTHER COCK, *pushing the others aside*
And I reject all previous theories and thoughts:
Coo-doo-kuckle-kak!
                    long pause
                              Coo! My song's
A free and urbane blend of noise and chance.

                         CHANTECLER
I think I'm going insane.

                    THE COCK, *shouting*
                              Urbane!

                         CHANTECLER
                                        Insane!

          ALL THE COCKS, *around him, fighting among themselves*
Cock... no, Cawk... No, no, Ko-kay... Uh-OO...

CHANTECLER
Which one to believe?

THE COCK WHOSE SONG IS A BLEND
The free and urbane crow
Is obligatory!

CHANTECLER
Who is speaking with such
Authority?

1st CHICKEN
A marvellous Cock who's never
Crowed at all.

CHANTECLER, *humbly, in despair*
And I'm just a Cock who has.

EVERYONE, *disgustedly, moving away*
Oh, well. . .

CHANTECLER
I dare to give my song, as a rosebush
Gives its rose.

PEACOCK, *sarcastically*
I knew we'd get to the Rose.

Pitying laughter.

CHANTECLER
nervously, aside to the Blackbird
You think my killer will keep me dangling here
Much longer?

EVERYONE, *disgustedly*
Oh, the Rose. . .

GUINEA HEN, *nauseated by such banality*
Please talk of flowers
Less. . .

PEACOCK
Plebeian.
with the most contemptuous insolence
You decline *Rosa*?

CHANTECLER

I do, you... Peacock! Still, I suppose I must
Forgive you for daring to speak so slightingly
Of the rose, *rosae*, because, poor fireworks-maker,
There's no contest: Next to her, your fire
Is just a flash in the pan.

looking around him

I call on all
You Cocks to help me while I defend her.

A COCK, *negligently*

Whom?

CHANTECLER

The Rose, *rosam*; to say right here and now...

BLACKBIRD

You call yourself a champion, then?

CHANTECLER

I do,

Of roses, *rosarum*... to say that one must worship...

A COCK

Whom?

CHANTECLER

The roses, *rosas*, where the rain
Can sleep as sweet as if inside a vase;
To say they always are and will be—

A VOICE, *cold and cutting*

Trash!

*All the exotic Cocks draw aside, revealing
at the back, between their rows, the White Pile—
tall, lean, and sinister.*

CHANTECLER

At last.

BLACKBIRD

It's time to climb on the seats.

CHANTECLER, *to the White Pile*

Look here...

PHEASANT

You're not going to challenge that giant?

                          CHANTECLER
                                        Talking down
Is all it takes to make one tall.
                  crossing to the White Pile
                                                Remarks
Like yours can't be allowed...
                  Finding a Chick between himself and the
                  White Pile, he puts it aside, saying
                                        Run back to the crowd.
      to the White Pile, insolently eyeing his clipped comb
You look like a cockatoo cut down to one.

                  WHITE PILE, *dumbfounded*
Cockatoo? Cut? What? What?

                  CHANTECLER, *beak to beak with him*
What? What? What?
            A pause. They stare at each other, ruffs bristling.

                  WHITE PILE, *with emphasis*
                                    On my last tour
I killed three Cornish Blues in one day. I've killed
Two Gingers, three Sumatras, a Mealy Gray.
I've killed—that's why they never fight me without
First drinking something to keep the fever away—
Five Red Duns in Phoenix and ten in L. A.

                  CHANTECLER, *simply*
I've never killed a thing. But sometimes I
Have had to protect and defend my realm, so maybe
I am brave in my own way. Don't act
The king of the molehill with me: I came here knowing
You would come. I dangled that rose to give you
A chance for brute stupidity. You didn't
Fail to grab the petals. What's your name?

                  WHITE PILE
White Pile. And yours?

                  CHANTECLER
Is Chantecler.

                  PHEASANT, *running to the dog*
                                        Patou!

                  CHANTECLER
            proudly, as Patou snarls between his teeth
Stay out of this!

PATOU, *rolling his r's*
That's harrrd, my frrriend.

PHEASANT, *to Chantecler*
But why

Should a Cock face death for a rose?

CHANTECLER
An attack on a flower

Attacks the Sun; they have identical foes.

PHEASANT, *running to the Blackbird*
You promised me that all was well.

BLACKBIRD
And so

It is. Except for fights between friends.

GUINEA HEN, *uttering cries of despair*
Oh, no!

A garden party where they kill each other!
Dreadful...
     to her son
          ...that the Turtle hasn't arrived.

A VOICE
It's ten to one on Chantecler!

GUINEA HEN, *helping Hens to climb on the flower pots,*
pumpkins, and seats
Be quick!

BLACKBIRD
She's hopped up—hostessing hostilities.

A big circle forms. In the second row are the exotic Cocks;
in front, avid, all the barnyard Hens, Chicks, and Ducks.

PATOU, *to Chantecler*
Go win! The public wants to see your guts!

CHANTECLER, *sadly*
I always treated them well.

PATOU
indicating the expectant, hate-filled circle
Just look.

All the necks are extended, all the eyes shining.
It is hideous. Chantecler looks, realizes, and lowers his head.

PHEASANT

The sluts!

CHANTECLER, *straightening*
All right! At least today they'll know who I am
And what my secret is.

PATOU

No! Not if
It's what this old idealist has guessed.

CHANTECLER, *addessing them all in a ringing voice, chest
lifted like someone about to confess his faith*
Know, then, that I'm the one...
There is a terrible silence.
to the White Pile, who gestures impatiently
I'm sorry, but
I wish to do one thing that's brave before
I face the hereafter.

WHITE PILE, *surprised*
Oh?

CHANTECLER

Face their laughter.

PHEASANT

No!

CHANTECLER
Let a jeer be the last thing I hear!
to the crowd
Get ready,
You who learn from the Blackbird!
in a voice that keeps rising with strain
I'm the one
Whose song each day calls back the light to your sky.
Stupefaction. Then a huge laugh shakes the crowd.
The whole world's laughing? Then, en garde!

GOLDEN POLISH COCK

Let's go!

The fight begins.

VOICES HEARD AMID THE GALES OF LAUGHTER
It's a scream! — A riot! — Cracked me up! — Convulsed me!

A HEN

He calls the daylight!

A DUCK
Daylight comes when he calls!

CHANTECLER, *avoiding the White Pile's blows*
Yes, I'm the one who brings you back the light.

A CHICK

And how!

CHANTECLER
solemnly, while thrusting and parrying
The songs of other cocks don't bring
Anything to birth or death; that's why they're just
Great wastes of breath. But mine...
He sustains a wounding blow.

A VOICE
Pow! On the neck!

CHANTECLER

...Calls up...

Another wound.

TURKEY

Such ego!

CHANTECLER
The Li...
He is hit again.

A VOICE
Pow! On the beak!

CHANTECLER

...The Li...

A VOICE
Pow! In the eye!

CHANTECLER, *haggard, blinded by blood*
...calls up the Light!

A MOCKING VOICE
Know what that makes you? An obscurantist.

CHANTECLER
repeating mechanically under the blows
It's I who call the Dawn.

PATOU, *barking*
                    Yes, yes!

PHEASANT, *sobbing*
                                              Hit back!

A CHICKEN
My friends, let's give the Dawn a nickname.

ALL, *stamping their feet*
                                              Yes!

The White Pile hurls himself at Chantecler.

PHEASANT
What a shock!

BLACKBIRD, *offering the requested nickname*
The Call Girl.

A VOICE
Now a name for the Cock.

ALL, *stamping*
Yes, yes!

BLACKBIRD
The Sunshine Boy!

ANOTHER VOICE
                                    Arson Welles!

CHANTECLER, *defending himself step by step*
Another pun—because I still can move.

A VOICE
The Alarm Cock!

CHANTECLER
who seems sustained only by the insults
More! And I know nothing of war
But barnyard scuffles—how to bite and kick...

A VOICE
...The bucket!

CHANTECLER
Thank you! I...

His torn feathers fly around him.

A JOYFUL CRY
He's being plucked!

CHANTECLER

...I feel... —More jokes!

A CHICK
You feel *light*-headed, maybe?

CHANTECLER

Thanks!... —I feel that the more you laugh and chaff
And scoff and boff and guffaw...

A DONKEY, *putting its head over the hedge*
Hee-haw!

CHANTECLER

Thanks!

—The more I'll learn to fight.

WHITE PILE, *sneering*
Oh, he can fight,

But he's all done in.

PHEASANT, *begging*
Enough!

A VOICE
On the White Pile, four

To one!

PHEASANT, *seeing Chantecler's bleeding throat*
He's bleeding.

A HEN, *on tiptoe behind the Golden Polish Cock*
Let me see the blood!

WHITE PILE, *furiously driving deeper*

I'll skin him alive!

THE HEN WHO WANTS TO SEE
This Polish hat's in the way.

BLACKBIRD

Hats off!

Chantecler seems lost; he curls in a ball as if to die.

A VOICE
What a blow—on the comb!

CRIES FROM THE DELIRIOUS CROWD
Rip it off! Slit his throat!
Kill him!

PATOU, *standing on his wheelbarrow*
You know what you sound like? Human beings.

RHYTHMIC CRIES
matching the blows Chantecler receives
In the eye! — On the head! — On the wing! — On the. . .

Sudden silence.

CHANTECLER
What? They break
Their circle and stop their noise?
*He looks around. The White Pile has stopped his attack
and pulled back against the hedge. There is a strange motion
in the crowd. Exhausted, bleeding, stumbling, Chantecler
doesn't grasp what is happening and murmurs:*
What new attack
Do they plan?
suddenly, very moved
Patou, it's wonderful.

PATOU
What is?

CHANTECLER
I slandered them: They've stopped their jeering talk
And now they're coming close to me.

PATOU
*seeing that everyone, while approaching Chantecler, watches
the sky uneasily, he lifts his head, looks, and says simply*
It's the Hawk.

CHANTECLER
Ah.

*A shadow passes slowly over the crowd, which shrinks
together and instinctively moves closer and closer
to Chantecler.*

PATOU
When that great shadow blots their sun,
It's not to fancy foreign Cocks that they run.

CHANTECLER
Suddenly erect and growing taller, his wounds forgotten,
he stands in their midst and says commandingly
Come now, gather close.

PHEASANT
Dear brave and gentle soul.

The shadow passes over again. The Fighting Cock
shrinks. In the heap of ruffled, trembling feathers,
only Chantecler is left standing.

A HEN, *her eyes following the Hawk's progress*
That's twice already the shadow has blackened our day.

CHANTECLER, *calling some Chicks who run about distractedly*
This way, you Chicks!

PHEASANT
You take them under your wing?

CHANTECLER
I must. Their mother is artificial.

The shadow of the Hawk, making ever lower circles,
passes over a third time, even blacker.

PHEASANT
Oh,

It hovers.

ALL, *moaning in terror*
Ah!

CHANTECLER, *sending a ringing cry to the sky*
I'm here!

PATOU
It hears your trumpet...

PHEASANT
Flies away...

The shadow has passed.

ALL, *standing up, with a joyous shout*
Ah!

They run to take up their places for the end of the fight.

PATOU

And once again

The circle forms.

CHANTECLER
What's that?

PHEASANT

They want to see
You killed, to make you pay for the fear they felt.

CHANTECLER
But now I won't be killed. My strength rose high
The moment our common Enemy filled the sky.
He marches on the White Pile.
Trembling for others has brought my courage back.

WHITE PILE, *astounded by being vigorously attacked*
This sudden strength...?

CHANTECLER

Is three times more than yours!
I react to the sight of black like a bull to red,
And I've just seen Night three times in a shadow overhead.

*Cornered against the hedge, the White Pile
prepares to use his knives.*

PHEASANT
Watch out! He's got two spurs of very sharp steel.

CHANTECLER

I knew it!

CAT, *from his tree, to the White Pile*
Use your razors.

PATOU, *ready to spring from his wheelbarrow*

Do, and I

Will strangle you!

CROWD, *disappointed*
Oh, no...

PATOU

Despite your cries.

WHITE PILE, *feeling that he's lost*
So much the worse.

PHEASANT, *whose eyes never leave him*
He's turned one razor up!

WHITE PILE, *striking with his sharp spur*
Take this and die!

He gives a terrible cry, while Chantecler,
leaping aside, avoids the blow.
Aaaahh...

He collapses. There is a cry of astonishment.

SEVERAL VOICES
What happened?

BLACKBIRD, *who has hopped over to see*

Nothing.
Just that his right foot cut his left.

THE CROWD
following and jeering the White Pile, who, having
painfully raised himself, hops off on one leg

Boo!

PATOU AND PHEASANT
laughing, crying, and speaking all at once, beside
Chantecler, who is motionless and spent, his eyes closed
Chantecler! — It's us! — The Dog! The Pheasant!
Talk to us!

CHANTECLER
opens his eyes, looks at them, and says softly
Tomorrow the day will dawn.

THE CROWD
having led the White Pile off, comes back eagerly
and admiringly to Chantecler

Hurray!

CHANTECLER, *starts; then in a terrible voice*
Stay back! I've seen you for what you are.

The crowd pulls back quickly.

PHEASANT, *leaping to his side*
Then come to the woods—see animals who are real.

CHANTECLER
I'm staying here.

PHEASANT
Knowing what they're like?

CHANTECLER

Yes, knowing.

PHEASANT
And still you'd stay?

CHANTECLER
But not for them—
For my song. It might burst forth less clearly once
I stood on different soil. And now, to tell
The Day she'll once again be born, I'll sing.
The crowd obsequiously starts to move toward him.
Stay back! I've nothing left but my song.
All pull back, and alone with his pride, he begins.
Cock...
to himself, stiffening against pain
Except my song. So let's sing well.
He starts again.
Cock... Is it placed in my chest? Or... Cock... in my head?
And how do I scan? Co... ckadoo... And the accent?
COCK... cockaDOO... I can't get started... Cawker...
Since they've got me thinking... Ko-kay... The scheme?
Cock...
in anguish
I'm all ensnared in rules and schools!
Their way of flying would bring an eagle down.
He gives a last, abortive try, which ends in a hoarse sound.
Cock... I can't anymore. I've lost it—I
Who sang not knowing how but only why.
desperately
I've nothing left! They took it—even my song.
How can I find it again?

PHEASANT, *opening her wings to him*
Come to the woods.

CHANTECLER, *falling on her breast*

I love you.

PHEASANT
No one there ensnares birds' voices.

CHANTECLER

Yes, let's go.

>   *He moves with her to the rear,*
>   *but turns back before leaving*
>   But first I have a word...

>   PHEASANT, *trying to lead him away*
Come to the woods.

>   CHANTECLER
>   ...For all the Guinea Hennites
Gathered beneath these arbors: Leave the garden—
I'm sure the Bees would agree—to do its work
Of turning flowers into fruit.

>   BUZZING OF BEES
>   *So true! So true!*

>   CHANTECLER
No good is ever achieved in the midst of noise.
Noise prevents the branch...

>   BUZZING, *moving away*
>   *So true! So true!*

>   CHANTECLER
...From giving its apple a perfect shine; the grape...

>   BUZZING, *lost among the leaves*
So true!

>   CHANTECLER
>   ...From turning ripe on its arbor-vine.
>   *moving to the rear with the Pheasant*
Let's go.
>   *turning back angrily*
>   I've one more thing to say to all
These Pro—
>   *The Pheasant puts her wing over his beak.*
>   —per hens: The fancy Cocks will run
Right back to the troughs they've grown to need as soon
As someone cries,
>   *He imitates someone scattering grain.*
>   "Here, chick, chick, chick!" Because
Those charlatans have nothing but legs and a stomach.

>   PHEASANT, *pulling him*
Come. Come on!

>   A HEN
>   She's abducting him.

CHANTECLER

That's right.

coming back
I've something to say to this Peacock...
indicating the Guinea Hen
In front of this pea-brain.

GUINEA HEN, *enchanted*
Insulted right in my home! Sensational!

CHANTECLER, *to the Peacock*
You blustering bully whom Fashion took for a guide,
You walk in the fear, with which your throat is blue,
Of not being up-to-date in the eyes of your Queue;
But, constantly pushed by all those eyes, you'll fall,
And you and your false artistry will end
With the false immortality conferred by the...
imitating the Peacock's way of speaking
Shall

I say, the stuffer of birds?

GUINEA HEN, *mechanically*
Yes!

CHANTECLER

No!

The taxidermist, to use the word that you
Would choose.

BLACKBIRD
Touché!

CHANTECLER, *turning on him*
And as for you...

BLACKBIRD

Fire away.

CHANTECLER
I will.
moving down
You told us that one pale day you met
A city sparrow. That was the ruin of you.
For ever since, you're gripped by the fear of not
Being "citified" enough.

BLACKBIRD
But I...

CHANTECLER

I'm talking!
Unaware that a mocking whistle never
Can be a cheer from the Bronx, you've put your feet,
You country bird, as if they touched concrete.
And so...

BLACKBIRD

But I...

CHANTECLER

I'm not done firing yet!
...Sparrowing day and night, and even while
You sleep, you condemn yourself to sparrow for life,
But trying to become a sparrow has made you an ass.

BLACKBIRD

But I...

CHANTECLER

Oh, touching efforts of a farmyard bird
To twist his beak and speak like a street-wise cynic!
Slang is what you want to reap? Each bite
You take explodes in your jaw, for city grapes
Are bubbles of glass. You took from the sparrow only
His tricks and smirks, which makes you nothing but
An under-clown, a second banana, dressed
In a coarse tuxedo, pulling cheap tricks from old hats.
You serve us stale old skepticisms found
With the crumbs on a barroom floor. Poor little bird,
Who thinks his second-hand tales will scandalize.
        to one of the exotic Cocks, chattering behind him
Be quiet there, you Japanese! Or else
I'll cut your cackle-mono down to size!

JAPANESE COCK

Excuse me, please...

CHANTECLER, *to the Blackbird*
You'd like to imitate
The Sparrow, he who spreads his wings when he laughs
And underlines his words on a telephone wire?
I hate upsetting you, but I have heard
The sparrows while they steal my grain, and you
Aren't with it at all. Your satire's bunk. It's bogus.

BLACKBIRD, *astounded*
Slang from you?

CHANTECLER
Your wit is counterfeit—
The genuine article made in Hong Kong.

BLACKBIRD
                                                              What's
All this? He's using jokes to slap me down?

CHANTECLER
The best of mockers is a singer who plays the clown.

BLACKBIRD
But I. . .

CHANTECLER
You told me to fire away. Does it burn?

BLACKBIRD
I. . .

CHANTECLER
The Chief of Light-Rays, here to serve you.
Were you saying something?

BLACKBIRD
                                No.
                                        He tries to get away.

CHANTECLER
                                                              You'd like
To imitate the city sparrow? Learn
That his jokes are not a way of sitting on the fence,
Of having no opinion and never giving any offense.
His eye either glares or glows; it's always lit!
And now you want the key that winds up his wit?
You want the secret by which this urchin steals
Our hearts with a mocking quip? It's that he *feels*
When he scoffs; beneath his street-wise repartee
Is a soul. The secret is that he's proud and free,
And a fire escape, where a child has laid out crumbs,
Is the only place that ever briefly becomes
His cage in the open sky. It's that one knows
He has a survivor's soul because he chose
To face down hunger and poverty with a jest.
You want to imitate this fool whose nest
Is built sky-high on a tower of glass and concrete?
One must take risks to be a child of the street!
But you, whose wit lacks love and therefore fun,

You think that spite replaces satire, that one
Becomes a clown by wearing a cowardly sneer,
That we're so dumb and deaf we'll never hear
The difference between your black-hearted jokes and slings
And a flash of genuine wit from a heart that sings!
Now, pull yourself out of that—if you've got wings.

GUINEA HEN

who approves everything said at her affairs

Very good!

A CHICK, *to the nonplussed Blackbird*
You'll make him pay?

BLACKBIRD, *prudently*

I'll take it out

On the Turkey.

A VOICE CALLS
Here, chick, chick, chick, chick!

*All the exotic Cocks rush to the irresistible
sound of food, tumbling over each other.*

GUINEA HEN, *running after them*

You're leaving?

A PADUA, *the last to go*

Sorry. . .yes.

He disappears.

GUINEA HEN, *in the midst of the uproar*
They're going! Everyone's going!

CHANTECLER, *to the Pheasant*

Come, my Pheasant of the wilds.

GUINEA HEN

You're running away?

CHANTECLER

To save my song.

GUINEA HEN, *running to the Guinea Cock*
Oh, son, I'm in *such* a state!

A HEN, *crying to Chantecler*

But when will you be back?

CHANTECLER
When you have teeth!

He leaves, with the Pheasant.

GUINEA HEN, *to the Guinea Cock*
Today was the best affair there ever has been.
dashing about among the last guests to leave
Goodbye! —Till next time! —See you then!

MAGPIE, *announcing*
The Turtle!

The curtain falls.

ACT FOUR

The Night
of the Nightingale

THE SCENE: In the middle of the forest.

The green asylum sought by all disappointed hearts. The shadow that simplifies and the peace that soothes. Under giant oaks whose age is no longer known, roots spread out their hunchbacked spurs.

A passing of squirrels. A glimpse of rabbits. In the vales where colt's-foot grows, mushrooms sometimes gather into villages. Acorns fall soundlessly on the waiting moss.

Night. A stream. A bindweed. How far away is the world! From the tips of some heather to the points of a fern, the spider has stretched her ornamental snare.

Held in its threads is a swelling, oval drop of rain; one might think she had caught a crystal ladybird.

AT RISE: Throughout the underbrush, as far as can be seen, RABBITS are taking in the night air. A moment of silence and freshness.

A RABBIT
Now is the time when two songbirds—blackcap
Of the garden and browncoat who comes from the reeds—will slowly
Say the evening prayer.

A VOICE, *in the branches*
O God of Birds!

ANOTHER VOICE
Or rather—so we're sure of being heard,
For the vulture's God is not the same as the lark's—
O God of Little Birds!

THOUSANDS OF VOICES, *in the leaves*
Of Little Birds!

FIRST VOICE
Who filled our bones with air to make us rise
And gave our feathers colors torn from the skies,
We offer thanks for the lovely day, for the creek
We drink, for the grains we pick with a tiny beak,
For giving us the sharp little eyes that find
All man's invisible foes, for having designed
Such good little tools for us, as gardeners born:
Our pruners and clippers of black or yellow horn...

SECOND VOICE
Tomorrow we'll do battle with thistle and blight:
Forgive us, please, for the venial sins of tonight—
For yielding to the sweet temptation of a berry or two.

FIRST VOICE
We offer thanks for the sleep you bring; when you
Breathe soft upon our eyes, their three lids close.
O Lord, if the stones that unjust Mankind throws
Are all we reap for the carpet of song we spread
And the battle we do with weevils to save his bread,
If all our family is caught one day in his snares,
Then bring Saint Francis of Assisi into our prayers;
We must forgive men's painful nets and words
Because one man has said, "My brothers the birds."

SECOND VOICE, *as if speaking a litany*
And you, great Francis, Saint who blessed our wings...

THOUSANDS OF VOICES, *in the leaves*
Pray for us!

THE VOICE
Priest of All that Sings,
Confessor of Finches...

ALL THE VOICES
Pray for us!

THE VOICE
Dreamer
Who believed in a soul for us, Redeemer
Whose belief has stirred that soul to life...

ALL THE VOICES
Pray for us!

FIRST VOICE
Keep us from hunger and strife,
O blessed Francis, show us where and when
To find our grains of barley...

SECOND VOICE
And wheat...

ANOTHER VOICE
And millet!

FIRST VOICE

Amen!

ALL
in a murmur that runs through the whole forest
Amen!

CHANTECLER
who has just appeared from the hollow of a large tree
Amen!

*The shadows have grown bluer. A ray of moon strikes
the spider's web, which seems to be sifting silver dust.
The Pheasant leaves her tree and follows Chantecler
with little steps.*

CHANTECLER
Now the ferns
Are drenched in moonlight, now. . .

A LITTLE TREMBLING VOICE
At Night Hope is bright.

PHEASANT

Thanks, Spider.

CHANTECLER

Now. . .

PHEASANT, *close behind him*
You can kiss me, now!

CHANTECLER
With all those rabbits watching, it's awkward.

PHEASANT
*beats her wings. The frightened rabbits disappear;
on all sides white tails are swallowed up in the burrows.
Returning to Chantecler:*
There.

They kiss.
You love my forest?

CHANTECLER
Dearly. The moment I
Came near, my song returned. And now let's go
To roost. Tomorrow I must sing quite early.

PHEASANT, *imperious*

Just one song!

> CHANTECLER
> Yes.

> PHEASANT
>
> > > One song is all

I've allowed, all month.

> CHANTECLER, *resigned*
> Yes.

> PHEASANT
>
> > > Does the Sun still rise?

> CHANTECLER, *grudgingly*

It does.

> PHEASANT
> You see that one may have the Dawn

At a smaller cost. Is the sky less red because
You sing just once?

> CHANTECLER
> No.

> PHEASANT
>
> > > Well, then?
> > > > *offers her beak*
> > > > A kiss...

Your heart wasn't in it. Look...

> > *returning to her theme*
> > > Why work so hard?

You waste your brass. The day is lovely, yes,
But one must live. Ah, men. If we weren't there,
How often you'd be fooled.

> CHANTECLER, *with conviction*
>
> > > But you are there.

> PHEASANT

Besides, when I'm asleep, it's barbarous
For you to cry a hundred times.

> CHANTECLER, *correcting gently*
>
> > > > Sweetheart,

It's "crow."

> PHEASANT
> Well, I've heard "cry."

CHANTECLER
It's "crow."

PHEASANT
looks to the top of the tree and calls

Professor!

to Chantecler
I'll ask the bird who wears a cap and gown.
*to the Woodpecker, the upper half of whose body
appears in a hole at the top of the tree. He has
a white vest and a black cap.*
Is "cry" correct? Or "crow"?

WOODPECKER, *lowering a long doctoral beak*
Both are.

CHANTECLER AND PHEASANT
turning to each other triumphantly

Aha!

WOODPECKER
"Cry" connotes more passion, "crow" more strength.

CHANTECLER
Sweetheart, for you I'll...cry.

PHEASANT
And then you'll "crow"

For the Dawn!

CHANTECLER
You're jealous, eh?

PHEASANT, *retreating coquettishly*
You love me more

Than Her?

CHANTECLER, *a warning*
Look out! A snare!

PHEASANT, *leaping aside*
Ready to fall!
Visible against the tree there is indeed a net.

CHANTECLER, *studying it*

It's dreadful.

PHEASANT
It's also against the wildlife statutes.

CHANTECLER, *laughing*
How, my dear, would you know that?

PHEASANT

You seem

To forget that you had the honor to fall in love
With a gamebird.

CHANTECLER, *a bit sadly*
True, we belong to different races.

PHEASANT, *going back to him with a leap*
Say you love me more than Her—say it's me.

WOODPECKER, *reappearing*

"It's I."

CHANTECLER, *lifting his head*
Not in a love scene, please.

PHEASANT, *to the Woodpecker*

Listen,

You, knock before you enter.

WOODPECKER, *disappearing*

Oh,

All right.

PHEASANT, *to Chantecler*
He's quite a busy-beak, but still,
He's a noted scholar.

CHANTECLER
Of what?

PHEASANT

Of the language of birds.

CHANTECLER

Oh, yes?

PHEASANT
Although birds pray in verse, you know,
Among themselves in the woods they use a limpid
Onomatopoeic dialect.

CHANTECLER

They speak Japanese.

> *The Woodpecker gives three little knocks*
> *on the tree with his beak.*
> Come in.

> WOODPECKER, *appears, indignant*
> Japanese?

> CHANTECLER
> That's right.

"Tio! Tio!", or some say "Tooee! Tooee!"

> WOODPECKER

Birds, since Aristophanes, have spoken
Greek.

> CHANTECLER, *running to the Pheasant*
> Oh, for the love of Greek...
> *They kiss.*

> WOODPECKER
> Know,

Irreverent youth, that the warbler's mocking cry
Of "Wee-wees-tra-tra" comes, corrupted, straight
From the Greek word Lysistrata.

> *He disappears.*

> PHEASANT, *to Chantecler*
> Say you'll never

Love a soul but me.

> *Three knocks are heard.*

> CHANTECLER
> Come in!

> PHEASANT, *to Chantecler*
> You swear it?

> WOODPECKER, *appearing, shaking his head*
"Tiri-para," song of the thrush in the reeds.
It comes from the Greek: "*Para*, along." "The water"
Is understood.

> *He disappears.*

> CHANTECLER, *to the Pheasant*
> He's got Greek on the brain.

PHEASANT
And the skullcap keeps it there.
returning to her theme
Tell me, am I
All things to you?

CHANTECLER
Of course! Although...

PHEASANT
How
Do I seem to you, in my Oriental robe with sleeves
Of green?

CHANTECLER
Like a living order always to adore
Whatever comes from the East.

PHEASANT, *beginning to lose control*
Leave your uncertain
Dawn for one you're more sure to find—in my eyes.

CHANTECLER
I'll never forget that there was a morning when
We shared a belief in my destiny, and you,
In that glorious hour when love was born, surrendered
Your own gold to the Dawn.

PHEASANT, *impatient*
Oh, the Dawn!
Watch out, or I'll do something foolish.

She moves away.

CHANTECLER, *dryly*
Do.

PHEASANT
The last time I was in the glade I met—

She stops herself, intentionally.

CHANTECLER, *a cry*
The Pheasant Cock?
with sudden violence
Swear not to go to the glade
Again!

PHEASANT, *feeling she has him, leaps toward him*
Swear to love me more than the Dawn!

CHANTECLER, *sadly*

Oh...

PHEASANT
Swear not to sing any more...

CHANTECLER

Than one song!

I've already sworn.
Three knocks are heard.
Come in.

WOODPECKER
appearing and indicating the net with his beak
That snare was laid

By the farmer. He said he'd take the Pheasant-Hen...

PHEASANT

He flatters himself.

WOODPECKER, *to the Pheasant*
And keep you on the farm.

PHEASANT, *indignant*

Alive?
reproachfully, to Chantecler
Your farm!

CHANTECLER
seeing a Rabbit who has reappeared on the sill of his burrow
Oh look, a rabbit is back.

RABBIT
to the Pheasant, indicating the net
You see, you put your foot on the spring...

PHEASANT, *in a superior tone*

And the thing

Snaps down. I know all about it, child. But I
Don't fear anything but dogs.
to Chantecler
The farm that you miss!

CHANTECLER, *in a tone of outraged innocence*

Who, me?

PHEASANT
to the Rabbit, giving him a tap of the wing to send him away
Nothing but dogs. And that reminds me,
I should go confound their noses by mixing
Up my tracks in the grass and the brush.

CHANTECLER
Yes, go
Confound their noses.

PHEASANT, *starts to leave, then returns*
Do you miss that farm?

CHANTECLER
Me? Me?
She leaves. He repeats indignantly
Me?
He watches her. Then, softly to the Woodpecker
She's not coming back?

WOODPECKER
who can see far, from the top of his tree
No.

CHANTECLER
Keep watch. I'm getting news from home!

WOODPECKER, *curious*
From whom?

CHANTECLER
The Blackbird.

WOODPECKER
I thought he hated you.

CHANTECLER
Almost. But a Blackbird mind can always change.
Besides, it amuses him to keep me in touch.

WOODPECKER, *astonished*
He's coming?

CHANTECLER
quite different since the Pheasant left:
light, almost playful
No. But the blue convolvulus
That climbs his cage among the wistaria
Communicates, by subterranean roots,

With the white convolvulus at the edge of the stream.
> *He moves toward it.*

So that by speaking into the calyx...
> *He plunges his beak into one of the trembling, milky trumpets.*

Hello!

CHANTECLER
Hello! Blackbird?

WOODPECKER, *nodding, to himself*
From the Greek: *Allos*, another. One speaks with another.

CHANTECLER
Hello! Blackbird?

WOODPECKER, *keeping watch*
You're quite imprudent, choosing
From all the convolvuli the one—

CHANTECLER
> *more and more happy, moving back to the Woodpecker*

The only
One that's open all night. When the Blackbird answers,
The bee who sleeps in the flower wakes up, and we—

THE BEE IN THE CONVOLVULUS
Frrrt!

CHANTECLER, *running to the flower*
The Bee!
> *finishing his thought, to the Woodpecker*

...And we convolvulate.

WOODPECKER, *shocked by the neologism*
Convolvulate?

CHANTECLER, *listening in the horn of the flower*
Oh? This morning?

WOODPECKER, *curious*
What?

CHANTECLER, *his voice filled with sudden emotion*
Thirty chicks were born.
> *listening again*

Briffaut is sick?
> *as if something interfered with his hearing*

Those Dragonflies! Their wings make static.
> *He cries:*

Ladies,
Please don't cut us off!
> *He listens.*

Big Jules has made
Patou go poaching?
>   *to the Woodpecker*
If you just knew Patou...
>   *plunges back into the flower*
Oh, really? Things go badly without me?... Yes...
>   *with satisfaction*
A mess...

CHANTECLER
>   *On the lookout, he cries suddenly in a low voice:*
The Pheasant!

CHANTECLER, *still in the flower*
Oh?

WOODPECKER, *fluttering desperately*
Stop!

CHANTECLER

The Ducks
Spent all night under the cart?

WOODPECKER
Pssst!

PHEASANT
entering, to the Woodpecker with a menacing gesture

Get out!

>   *The Woodpecker retreats precipitately.*
>   *She listens to Chantecler.*

CHANTECLER, *in the flower*
Oh, really? All?... Yes?... No?... Oh!

WOODPECKER, *reappearing timidly, aside*
A caterpillar should get his tongue.

CHANTECLER, *in the flower*

So soon?
The Peacock's out of style?

WOODPECKER
trying to warn him behind the Pheasant's back
Pssst!

PHEASANT, *turning around furiously*

You!

The Woodpecker retreats precipitately, bumping his head.

CHANTECLER, *in the flower*
An older Rooster? I hope the Hens...
with progressively reassured intonations
Ah, good...

Good... good!
He finishes with obvious relief.
A father.
as if answering a question
Do I sing?

Yes, but far from here, near some ponds.

PHEASANT
What's that?

CHANTECLER, *with a little bitterness*
Golden Pheasants won't admit
That bringing glory takes great effort, so
I have to call the dawn in secret.

PHEASANT, *coming up behind him threateningly*
Oh!

CHANTECLER
As soon as the eyes that intoxicate me....

PHEASANT, *stopping*
Ah....

CHANTECLER
Have closed and she's asleep, so sweetly...

PHEASANT, *delighted*
Ah...

CHANTECLER
I escape.

PHEASANT, *furious*
Oh!

CHANTECLER
I steal far away, through the dew,
To sing the number of songs required, and when
I feel the darkness trembling—yes, when only
One more song will cleave it apart—I speed
Back here without a sound and roost again.
I wake The Pheasant by singing close to her.
Betrayed by the Dew? Oh no...

                              He laughs.
                                          ... because with the sweep
Of a wing I wipe the silver evidence off
My feet.

                        PHEASANT, *behind him*
                    You wipe your feet?

                        CHANTECLER, *turning around*
                              Oh, oh...
                                  into the flower
                                          It's nothing...
No, I'll call you... later... Oooh.

                        PHEASANT, *violent*
                                          And so,
Not only do you want to hear that your
Old mistresses are faithful...

                        CHANTECLER, *evasively*
                              Oh...

                        PHEASANT
                                          You even...

                        CHANTECLER
I...

                  BEE IN THE CONVOLVULUS
              Frrrt!

                  CHANTECLER, *putting his wing over the flower*
                        I...

                  BEE, *persisting under the wing*
                        Frrrt!

                        PHEASANT
                                          You cheat
So well you even think to wipe your feet!

                        CHANTECLER
But I...

                        PHEASANT
              One took a hayseed off his haystack;
Still one can't become the only one
In his soul.

CHANTECLER, *standing erect*
Believe me, when you live in a soul
It's better to meet the Dawn than to find it empty.

PHEASANT, *mutinous*
No! The Dawn robs me of love—a great love!

CHANTECLER
Great love exists in the shadow of a great dream only.
How can love not pour more freely from a heart
Whose work it is to open itself each day?

PHEASANT, *pacing angrily*
I'd like to lift my golden wing and sweep
Everything away.

CHANTECLER
And who are you, to do that?

They are reared against each other, looking defiance.

PHEASANT
The Pheasant Hen, who took the proud male's plumage.

CHANTECLER
Still, you're female, always seeing ideas
As rivals.

PHEASANT, *a cry*
Hold me next to your heart, and hush!

CHANTECLER
I'll hold you, yes, next to the heart of a Cock.
    with great regret
But how much better to hold you next to the soul
Of an Awakener.

PHEASANT
                                I was deceived
For the Dawn! All right, whatever the cost, deceive
The Dawn for me.

CHANTECLER
What?

PHEASANT
stamping her foot, speaking capriciously
                                I want you . . .

CHANTECLER, *appalled*

Listen...

PHEASANT

...To go one day without a song.

CHANTECLER

Me!

PHEASANT

I want you to go one day without a song!

CHANTECLER

Good God! to leave the darkness hanging over
The valley?

PHEASANT, *pouting*
Oh, what harm could it do the valley?

CHANTECLER

Things that stay too long in sleep and darkness
Grow too used to Lies and consent to Death.

PHEASANT

One day without a song.

insinuatingly

To remove my doubts.

CHANTECLER

I see what you're trying to do.

PHEASANT

I see what you fear.

CHANTECLER, *ardently*

I'll always sing!

PHEASANT

And if you're wrong? Suppose
The Dawn arrives without you?

CHANTECLER, *with fierce resolve*

I won't know it!

PHEASANT, *suddenly tearful*

Can't you forget the hour, when you see me crying?

CHANTECLER

No.

PHEASANT
Nothing can make you forget the hour?

CHANTECLER
No. The darkness weighs too heavily on me.

PHEASANT
The darkness? Shall I tell you the truth? You sing
In order to be admired. Crooner, go!
    with contemptuous pity
But your poor notes bring smiles to a forest that's used
To hearing the thrush's B flats.

CHANTECLER
                           You think you'll reach me
Through my pride.

PHEASANT
                   Your song could barely muster
Votes from four mushrooms and three mustard plants
When the thicket is pierced by the oriole's ardent cry
Of *"Pirpiriol"*...

WOODPECKER, *reappearing*
From the Greek: *"Puros*, pure."

CHANTECLER
Be quiet, you!

The Woodpecker disappears.

PHEASANT, *insistent*
               And what can the Echo think
Of you when he hears the splendid Nightingale?

CHANTECLER
You make me nervous.

He moves away.

PHEASANT
Have you heard him?

CHANTECLER
                                    Never.

PHEASANT
So enthralling are his songs that the very
First time one hears...

She stops, struck by an idea.
Oh!

CHANTECLER
What is it?

PHEASANT

Nothing.

to herself
So, the darkness weighs too heavily on you.

CHANTECLER, *moving back*
What's that?

PHEASANT, *with an ironic little curtsey*
It's nothing.
casually
Now let's go to roost.
Chantecler moves to do so. Then, to herself:
He doesn't know that whenever the nightingale
Sings in a sonorous wood, one thinks one has listened
For just five minutes, but the whole of the night has passed,
The way it does in a German fairy tale.

CHANTECLER
coming back down when she doesn't join him
What's that?

PHEASANT, *laughing in his face*
It's nothing.

A VOICE, *off*
Is that the Illustrious Cock?

CHANTECLER
Is someone asking for me?

PHEASANT
going to the side from the which the voice came
Over there, in the grass.

She recoils suddenly.
Dear Heaven, it's. . .
with a shudder
It's. . .
With a leap she hides in the hollow tree, calling
You talk to them.

A BIG TOAD, *rising up from the grass*

We've come...

Other Toads appear behind him.

CHANTECLER
Ye Gods! How ugly they are.

BIG TOAD, *obsequiously*

...To hail,

In the name of the Forest intellectuals,
The author of so many songs...

He has put his hand on his heart.

CHANTECLER, *in disgust*
Ugh, that hand

On his paunch.

BIG TOAD, *taking a little hop toward him*
...That are new!

ANOTHER TOAD, *same business*
Clear!

ANOTHER TOAD, *same business*
Vital!

ANOTHER TOAD, *same business*

Modern!

ANOTHER TOAD, *same business*

True!

CHANTECLER
Gentlemen, please sit down.

They sit around a large mushroom as if it were a table.

BIG TOAD

We're ugly, it's true...

CHANTECLER, *politely*
Your eyes are very nice.

BIG TOAD
hoisting himself up on the mushroom with both hands
But, as Knights of this Mushroom Round Table here,
We toast the Parsifal who's introduced
A song sublime.

SECOND TOAD
And true.

BIG TOAD
Celestial.

THIRD TOAD
Earthy.

BIG TOAD, *with authority*
Next to which the Nightingale is nothing.

CHANTECLER, *astounded*
Nightingale?

SECOND TOAD
He's nothing next to you.

CHANTECLER, *confused*
But sirs...

BIG TOAD, *with a little hop*
It was time for a new...

SECOND TOAD, *same business*
A new...

THIRD TOAD, *same business*
A new...

FOURTH TOAD
And different song...

FIFTH TOAD, *quickly, to his neighbor*
Above all, one that's foreign...

BIG TOAD
To change our culture.

CHANTECLER
Oh! I'll change your culture?

ALL
Hail to the Cock!

CHANTECLER, *more and more surprised*
The Forest looks more friendly.

BIG TOAD
The Nightingale is out.

CHANTECLER, *still more surprised*
Out?

SECOND TOAD
His song

Is just a trifle.

BIG TOAD
Philomelancholic.

THIRD TOAD

Nothing!

FOURTH TOAD, *contemptuously*
Sobs and throbs and trills. Passé.

FIFTH TOAD
And then, the name he uses: Bulbul!

ALL, *swelling with laughter, and hopping*
Bul-bul!

BIG TOAD
He goes like this:
    parodying the Nightingale's song
"Tio! Tio!"

SECOND TOAD
An ancient

Silver trill he plagiarized from the brook.
    He too imitates the Nightingale's song grotesquely.
"Tio!"

CHANTECLER
        But, look...

BIG TOAD, *quickly*
        Now, you're the avant-garde,
So don't defend that sentimental gargler.

SECOND TOAD
That worn-out tenor warbling all night long,
Just as if they'd never buried Keats.

THIRD TOAD
"My heart aches"—his precious cavatina.

CHANTECLER, *indulgently*
Well, if it amuses him, so what?

BIG TOAD
He uses every vocal trick there is.

CHANTECLER
Today, of course, we look for something more.

THIRD TOAD, *with finality*
Your song unmasks the artifice of his.

ALL, *exploding*
Down with Bulbul!

CHANTECLER
whom they have gradually surrounded
Dear Batrachians,
It's true my voice produces natural notes...

BIG TOAD
You make us all sprout wings!

CHANTECLER, *modestly*
Oh, well...

ALL, *wriggling as if about to fly*
Yes, wings!

BIG TOAD
You sing of Real Life.

CHANTECLER
Indeed...

SECOND TOAD
Yes, Life!

CHANTECLER, *carried away*
That's why my crest is made of flesh and blood.

ALL THE TOADS, *clapping their little hands*
Bravo! That's good!

BIG TOAD
Let's take it as our platform.

SECOND TOAD
Because it brings us all together, why not
Give the master...

CHANTECLER, *demurring*
Please...

                          SECOND TOAD
                                      ...whom we have lacked,
A banquet?

                              ALL
                  banging enthusiastically on the mushroom
                  Banquet!

              PHEASANT, *putting her head out of the tree*
                        What's going on?

                          CHANTECLER
                  a little flattered, in spite of it all

                                                    A banquet.

                      PHEASANT, *lightly ironic*

You accept?

                          CHANTECLER
                  Good Lord!... new trends in Art...
The Forest intellectuals...
                      indicating the Toads

                                                    I gave

Them wings...
        off-handedly
                  He's out, the Nightingale. Passé.
Sobs and trills. He goes...
                          to the Toads
                              How does he go?

                  ALL THE TOADS, *grotesquely*
"Tio! Tio!"

                          CHANTECLER
                  to the Pheasant, with indulgent pity
                      He goes "Tio! Tio!"
I think I can accept without a qualm...

                          A VOICE
                  *in the tree above him, sending forth
                      a long, moving, limpid note*

Tio!

                          Silence.

              CHANTECLER, *starting and lifting his head*
                  What was that?

BIG TOAD, *quickly and uneasily*
Nothing. Him.

THE VOICE
slowly and thrillingly, with the sigh of
a soul in each note
Tio!   Tio!   Tio!   Tio!

CHANTECLER, *turning on the Toads*
You toads!

THE TOADS, *backing away*
What?

NIGHTINGALE, *in the tree, in a throbbing voice*
Small and lost in the black of the tree,
I feel I'll become the infinite heart of the night.

CHANTECLER, *advancing on the Toads*
You dare compare. . .

THE TOADS, *recoiling*
But. . .

NIGHTINGALE
The ravine is wrapped in the spell
Of the moon.

CHANTECLER
. . .My crowing with that heavenly sound?
You toads! —I didn't see. They're doing here
To him what others did back there to me.

BIG TOAD, *suddenly puffing up*
Well, yes!

NIGHTINGALE
The mists are veils of trembling silk.

BIG TOAD, *self-importantly*
We are the Toads, our skins bedecked with warts!

They all rear up, swollen, between the tree and Chantecler.

CHANTECLER
I, who feel no envy, did not see
Their banquet would be laid with venom.

NIGHTINGALE
Never mind. You and I, the strong and tender,
We were meant to meet in spite of Toads.

CHANTECLER, *worshipfully*

Sing!

A TOAD
*who hastily drags himself to the foot of the tree
in which the Nightingale sings*
Let's smear the bark with our slimy little arms,
And drool at the foot of the tree.

They all crawl towards the tree.

CHANTECLER
trying to stop one who moves in clumsily
But Toad, don't you
Yourself have a nice singing voice?

THE TOAD, *in tones of the most sincere suffering*
Yes, but when
I hear another one, I drool with envy.

And he rejoins his brothers.

BIG TOAD
working his jaw as if there were scum in his mouth
Some kind of soap collects beneath our tongues,
And then...
to his neighbor
Do you drool?

THE OTHER
I drool.

ANOTHER
He drools!

ALL
We drool!

A TOAD
tenderly putting his arms around a loiterer's neck
Come drool.

CHANTECLER, *to the Nightingale*
But won't they stop your lovely song?

NIGHTINGALE, *proudly*

No. I take up their refrain. . .

BIG TOAD, *caressing a little one's head*

Come drool.

THE TOADS, *all together, crawling around the tree*

We are the Toads, the Toads are we.

NIGHTINGALE

. . .And make my song a Villanelle.

THE TOADS

We puff with pride and infamy.

NIGHTINGALE

And I, I burst with melody,
My throat must be a spouting well.

THE TOADS

We are the Toads, the Toads are we.

And the Villanelle proceeds with alternating voices,
the one carrying the melody growing ever higher and more
intoxicating; those carrying the refrain ever lower and more envious.

THE NIGHTINGALE AND THE TOADS, *alternating:*

I sing! Because the canopy
Of blue that forms my concert-shell,
—We puff with pride and infamy!—

The Night that whispers fervently,
The wind that swings the flower's bell,
—We are the Toads, the Toads are we!—

The love that knows my voice and key,
All pierce my senses, and compel. . .
—We puff with pride and infamy!—

. . .The soul that dark gods gave to me
To open up its citadel.
—We are the Toads, the Toads are we!—

All grief consigns her tears to me,
All tongues their dreams and legends tell. . .
—We puff with pride and infamy!. . .

I sing for all, eternally:
I am the Song you cannot quell!
—We are the Toads, the Toads are we!—

CHANTECLER, *caught up in the rhythm*
Beside this thrilling rhapsody
My song's as crude as Punch's yell.
Sing!... They flee, with...

THE TOADS
...infamy!

CHANTECLER
They go to simmer noxiously
In witches' cauldrons down in hell,
Because they are only...

THE TOADS, *already in the bushes*
...Toads are we!

CHANTECLER
But look! The beasts come openly
To drink the sound of your Villanelle.
They come in pairs. I see...

THE TOADS, *deep in the grass*
...-famy!

CHANTECLER
...A doe emerge, though cautiously,
Because she walks in parallel
To the stealthy pad of a wolf...

THE TOADS, *completely out of sight*
...are we!

CHANTECLER
The Squirrel clambers down the tree,
The Forest smiles beneath your spell.
Only the Echo remembers...

A DISTANT VOICE
...me!

CHANTECLER
The Toads, the Toads have ceased to be.
The song prevails, now no more than a song
without words, a shower of dazzling notes.

The glow-worms have lit their little belly-lamps;
All good comes forth, all hatred slinks away;
Those who will be eaten come to sit
In peace beside the eaters; suddenly
It seems that the Evening Star is not so far,
And the Spider leaves her lair, climbing up
To reach your song along her silken thread.

ALL THE FOREST, *in a long moan of ecstasy*
Ah!

The Forest lies as if enchanted; the moonlight is softer;
the soft green fires of the glow-worms wink among the moss;
and on all sides the charmed animals slip from among the trees,
muzzles lifted and eyes shining. The Woodpecker is at his bark
window, dreamily swinging his beak; and all the Rabbits,
with ears pricked, sit at their earthen doorways.

CHANTECLER
Squirrel, what do you hear in his wordless
Song?

SQUIRREL, *from his height*
The joy of leaping.

CHANTECLER
And you, Hare?

HARE, *in a copse*
The thrill of danger.

CHANTECLER
Rabbit, you?

ONE OF THE RABBITS
The dew.

CHANTECLER
And you, Doe?

DOE, *from the depths of the woods*
Tears.

CHANTECLER
And you, Wolf?

WOLF, *in a gentle, far-off howl*
The moon.

CHANTECLER
And you, the singing pine, tree
With the golden wound?

TREE
He tells me that my resin
Goes to sing on many bows.

CHANTECLER

Woodpecker,

You?

WOODPECKER, *in ecstasy*
He says that Aristophanes...

CHANTECLER, *interrupting quickly*
I know, I know! —Spider, you?

SPIDER, *rocking at the end of her thread*

He sings

Of the drop that glitter in my web like a lovely gift.

CHANTECLER
Glittering Raindrop, what does he tell you of?

A LITTLE VOICE, *coming from the web*
The Glow-worm.

CHANTECLER
Glow-worm, you?

A LITTLE VOICE, *in the grass*
The Star.

CHANTECLER

And you,

Star, if you'll permit me to ask?

A VOICE, *in the sky*
The Shepherd.

PHEASANT
who watches the horizon, between the trees
The darkness fades.

CHANTECLER
What kind of stream can it be
Where each one finds the water he needs to drink?
listening more attentively
To me he speaks of the day my song will bring.

PHEASANT, *to herself*
And speaks so well you're going to forget to bring it.

CHANTECLER
noticing a bird who has come slowly out of the thicket
and listens beatifically
Woodcock, how do you translate his poem?

WOODCOCK
I don't know. But it's ravishing.

PHEASANT, *constantly studying the sky*

It's pale.

CHANTECLER
to the Nightingale, in a discouraged voice
To sing!. . . But after hearing flawless crystal,
Can I be content with brass?

NIGHTINGALE

You must.

CHANTECLER
Will I be able to sing? I think I'll find
My song too red and brutal.

NIGHTINGALE

Sometimes mine
Has seemed to me to be too facile and blue.

CHANTECLER
Why should you confess such a thing to me?

NIGHTINGALE
Because you fought for a friend of mine, the Rose.
Keep this sad and reassuring thought,
That no-one, morning Cock or Nightingale,
Has quite the song of his dreams.

CHANTECLER, *with passionate yearning*
Oh, to be
A nocturne!

NIGHTINGALE
Oh, to be a call to work!

CHANTECLER
I can't bring tears.

NIGHTINGALE

I can't wake anyone up.

But after this moment of regret, he continues in a
voice that grows ever higher and more lyrical.

What does it matter! One must sing. Even

Knowing there are better songs to sing.

To sing until...

A shot. A flash in the thicket. Brief silence.
Then a little russet body falls at Chantecler's feet.

CHANTECLER, *bending down*

Oh, no!... The brutes!

And, without seeing the pale tremors that begin to
stir the air, he cries out in a sob.

Killed!

When he had only sung five minutes.

One or two feathers flutter slowly down.

PHEASANT

Look...

His feathers.

CHANTECLER, *as the body gives a last convulsion*

Die then, little poet.

The sound of leaves being trampled; from a bush
emerges Patou's large shaggy head.

You?

reproachfully

You've come for him?

PATOU, *ashamed*

The poacher makes me.

CHANTECLER, *who had leapt in front of the body*
to protect it, uncovers it.

It's

A nightingale!

PATOU, *hanging his head*

Yes. The wicked race

Loves to hurl its lead at a tree that sings.

CHANTECLER

Look there, the insect burial crew has come.

PATOU, *withdrawing gently*

I'll act as if I couldn't find a thing.

PHEASANT, *constantly watching the horizon*
He hasn't seen the night escape. . .

CHANTECLER
*leaning over the grasses, which begin to stir
around the little body.*

Beetles,

Quickly open the earth where the body fell.
—Necrophagans are the only grave-diggers who
Will never carry you elsewhere; they know
That the most pious, least sad tomb of all is the earth
Beneath you when you've fallen.

*to the funeral Insects, while the Nightingale
begins gently to sink into the ground*
Dig!

PHEASANT, *aside, watching the horizon*

Over there. . .

CHANTECLER
Bulbul will see the Bird of Paradise
Tonight.

PHEASANT
It's growing white.

A whistle is heard in the distance.

PATOU, *to Chantecler*
They're calling me.

But I'll be back.

He disappears.

PHEASANT
anxiously, watching first the horizon, then the Cock
How to hide it from him?
*She moves tenderly toward Chantecler, wings open,
to hide the lightening and to take advantage of his grief.*
Come and weep beneath my wing.
*With a sob he puts his head under the consoling wing,
which quickly folds over him. The Pheasant rocks him, murmuring:*
You see
How soft it is. . . You see. . .

CHANTECLER, *in a smothered voice*
Yes.

PHEASANT
continuing to rock him, darting glaces behind her
at the lightening sky

...That a wing

Is a heart spread open...
aside
Dawn arrives!
to Chantecler

That a wing...

aside
The tree is rose!
to Chantecler
...Is a shield that cradles, a cloak
That enfolds, a kiss that becomes a canopy...
You see...
She leaps back, and abruptly opening her wings:
That the day can rise without you!

CHANTECLER
with the greatest cry of sorrow a being can emit

No!

PHEASANT, *implacable*
That soon the mosses will turn scarlet!

CHANTECLER, *running to the moss*

No!

No, wait! Not without me!
The mosses flush red.
The ingrates.

PHEASANT

See

The horizon...

CHANTECLER, *begging it*
No!

PHEASANT
...Turn gold!

The whole upstage area does so.

CHANTECLER, *staggering*
What treachery!

PHEASANT
So one is all to a heart but nothing to a sky.

CHANTECLER, *defeated*
It's true.

PATOU, *returning, happily*
I'm back, it's me, I've come to say
That the whole farmyard is wild to see you, to admire
The Cock who stands on his slope and brings the Day!

CHANTECLER
They believe in me when I believe no longer.

PATOU, *stopping, astounded*
What?

PHEASANT, *pressing eagerly against Chantecler*
You see that a heart pressed close to yours
Is worth far more than a sky that doesn't need you.

CHANTECLER
Yes.

PHEASANT
That the dark is just as good as the Light
When deep in the darkness two are close.

CHANTECLER, *distracted*
Yes, yes . . .

*But suddenly he pulls away from her, stands erect,
and in a piercing voice:*
Cock-a-doodle-doo!

PHEASANT, *dumbfounded*
But why do that?

CHANTECLER
To warn myself, for three times I've denied
The thing I love.

PHEASANT
Which is?

CHANTECLER
My work.
to Patou
Come on,
Let's go!

PHEASANT
But what are you going to do?

CHANTECLER

My work.

PHEASANT, *furious*

What night is left to conquer?

CHANTECLER

That of the eyelid.

PHEASANT, *indicting the growing red of the Dawn*

So, you'll wake up sleepers—

CHANTECLER

Saint Peter, too!

PHEASANT

You've just seen day arise without your song.

CHANTECLER

My destiny is clearer than the day I see.

PHEASANT
*indicating the Nightingale's body, already
half-disappeared into the earth*

Your Faith can't be reborn, any more than he!

A VOICE
*in the tree, above their heads, suddenly sending
forth the moving, limpid notes*

Tio! Tio!

PHEASANT, *astounded*
Another song?

PATOU, *ears quivering*

Perhaps

An even better one.

PHEASANT
*looking with fright up into the leaves, then down
at the little grave*

Another song

When this one ends?

THE VOICE
The woods must always have

A nightingale.

CHANTECLER
And the soul, a faith so deep
In the grain that it comes back even after it's slain.

PHEASANT
But what if the sun is rising?

CHANTECLER
That's because
Some notes were left in the air from yesterday's song!

Soft, gray wings fly through the trees.

THE OWLS, *ululating joyfully*
Mute! He was mute!

PATOU, *lifting his head to follow them*
The Owls have fled the light
And come back into the forest.

OWLS, *regaining their holes in the old trees*
Mute! He was mute!

CHANTECLER, *all his strength returned*
There flies the proof that my song was serving the light:
The Owls are thrilled because they think I'm stilled!
   marching to the Pheasant, defiantly
I bring the Dawn, and I do more than that.

PHEASANT, *choking*
You what?

CHANTECLER
When animals awake on a day
That's gray and dare not believe in waking, then
The brass of my song stands in for the sun.
                              turning to leave
Let's sing!

PHEASANT
But how can one take heart when he doubts his work?

CHANTECLER
He sets to work with all his heart.

PHEASANT, *with stubborn anger*
But if
You're not the one who makes the morning come?

CHANTECLER

Then I'm the Cock of a still more distant sun.
My cries, in piercing the veil of Night, leave scars:
Those slits of daylight we all take for stars.
I'll never live to see the ultimate sky
That will light our roofs when all those stars draw nigh;
But if my song is always loud and clear,
And, clear and loud, when I'm no longer here,
If every farm has a Cock to attack the gray,
Then there'll be no more Night!

PHEASANT

Ah, when?

CHANTECLER

One Day!

PHEASANT

Go, then. Forget our forest.

CHANTECLER

Never. How
Could I forget the green and noble place
Which taught me that once you see a great dream die
You must either die at once or rise up stronger.

PHEASANT, *insultingly*

So, go climb your hen-house stairs like a king.

CHANTECLER

I've learned from the birds that one can climb with a wing.

PHEASANT

Go see that ancient Hen who lives in a basket.

CHANTECLER

Ah! Forest of Toad and Nightingales,
Of Pheasant and Poacher, once my old nurse sees
That I've come back from your cool glades, where love
And pain are mingled, what is she going to say?

PATOU, *imitating the affectionate old voice*

"He's grown."

CHANTECLER, *emphatically*

Of course.

He starts to leave.

PHEASANT
He's leaving... Oh, for arms
To hold them back when they're unfaithful, arms,
Arms! But we have only wings.

CHANTECLER, *stops and looks at her, troubled*
She's crying?

PATOU, *quickly*

Come!

CHANTECLER, *to Patou*
No, wait a minute.

PATOU
Sure. An old dog's
Good at watching tears.

PHEASANT
crying to Chantecler, leaping toward him
Take me with you!

CHANTECLER, *turns; in an inflexible voice*
You'll agree to stand second to the Dawn?

PHEASANT, *recoiling fiercely*
No, never!

CHANTECLER

Then goodbye.

PHEASANT
I hate you!

CHANTECLER
already at a distance in the brush
I adore you!
But I'd serve my calling badly, standing
Next to one who says there are greater things.

He disappears.

PATOU, *to the Pheasant*

Then cry...

SPIDER
in her web, which now sifts the gold of a ray of sun
Morning, warning.

PHEASANT
furious, breaking the web with a blow of her wing
Shut up, Spider!

—May he die for having left me! Oh!

WOODPECKER
who from his window has followed Chantecler's
departure; suddenly frightened

The Poacher sees him!

THE OWLS, *in the trees*
Now the Cock's in danger!

A YOUNG RABBIT
standing erect to see what the Poacher is doing

He breaks his gun in two.

AN OLD RABBIT
To load it up.

PATOU, *terrified*

That killer in sheepskin boots would fire at a Rooster?

PHEASANT, *opening her wings to fly*

Not if he sees a Pheasant.

PATOU, *leaping in front of her*
What will you do?

PHEASANT

My work!

She flies toward the danger.

WOODPECKER
seeing that in her flight she will touch the spring
of the forgotten snare
Look out for the net!

Too late. The net falls.

PHEASANT, *a desperate cry*
Oh!

PATOU
She's caught!

PHEASANT, *struggling in the mesh*

He's lost!

PATOU, *wildly*
Oh, she... But he...

All the rabbits have put out their heads.

PHEASANT, *crying an ardent prayer*
Protect him, Dawn!

OWLS, *hopping with joy on their branches*
The barrel glows! It's glowing!

PHEASANT
Touch the cartridge,
Dawn, with your wing! Make the hunter slip
On the dewy grass! Remember, he's your Cock!
Who banished the dark and chased away the hawk.
He's going to die! —Say something, Nightingale!

NIGHTINGALE, *in a beseeching sob*
He fought for a friend of mine, the Rose.

PHEASANT
Please let
Him live. I'll live in the barnyard, next to the plough.
And Sun, I'll admit—renouncing all those things
With which my pride has pained and burdened him—
That you marked out my place when you drew in
His shadow.

The day grows. Murmurs on all sides.

WOODPECKER, *singing*
The air is blue.

A CROW, *cawing in passing*
The day is growing.

PHEASANT
Everything awakes.

ALL THE BIRDS, *waking in the foliage*
Good morning! Morning!
Morning!

A JAY, *passing like a blue streak*
Ha! Ha! Ha!

WOODPECKER, *nodding*
That bluejay's laughter
Sounds Homeric.

PHEASANT
crying in the midst of all the morning stirrings
Let him live!

THE JAY, *passing again*

Ha! Ha!

A CUCKOO, *in the distance*

Cuckoo!

PHEASANT
I abdicate!

PATOU, *lifting his eyes to the sky*
She abdicates.

PHEASANT
Forgive me, Light to whom I dared dispute him.
Blind the wicked eye that's taking aim.
And morning Rays, please make your golden dust
The victor...
A shot. She screams.
Ah!
She finishes in a dying voice.
...over their black powder.

Silence.

CHANTECLER'S VOICE, *very far away*
Cock-a-doodle-doo!

ALL
He's safe!

THE RABBITS, *springing from their burrows*

Let's go
Turn somersaults in the thyme.

A VOICE, *fresh and solemn, in the trees*
O God of birds...

RABBITS, *stopping their somersaults, immobile*
The morning prayer.

WOODPECKER, *crying to the Pheasant*
They're coming to check the net!

PHEASANT, *closing her eyes, resigned*
So be it.

THE VOICE, *in the trees*
God for whom we . . .

PATOU
                      Sssh! Lower
The curtain, quick! Here come the human beings!

He leaves. All the animals hide. The Pheasant is
left alone. Wings open, breast heaving, crushed to the earth,
sensing the approach of the giant, she waits.

The curtain falls.

ABOUT THE TRANSLATOR

Kay Nolte Smith is a novelist whose first book, *The Watcher*, won an Edgar Allan Poe Award from the Mystery Writers of America. Her second novel, *Catching Fire*, set in the theater, reflects the years she spent as a professional actress. She has also written *Mindspell* and *Elegy for a Soprano*. Ms. Smith has taught writing and speech at Trenton State College and Brookdale Community College in New Jersey, and for the Education Department of AT&T Bell Laboratories. She is a *summa cum laude* graduate of the University of Minnesota and earned her MA in Speech and Theater at the University of Utah. She lives in Tinton Falls, New Jersey with her husband, Phillip J. Smith, a former professional actor and director who is now a Professor of Speech.